FAMILY ADVENTURE GUIDE™

NORTH CAROLINA

"The Family Adventure Guide series . . . enables parents to turn family travel into an exploration."
—Alexandra Kennedy, Editor, *FamilyFun* magazine

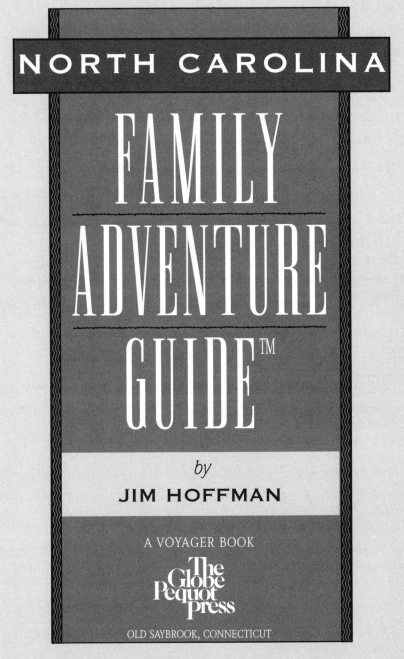

NORTH CAROLINA

FAMILY ADVENTURE GUIDE™

by

JIM HOFFMAN

A VOYAGER BOOK

The Globe Pequot Press

OLD SAYBROOK, CONNECTICUT

Family Adventure Guide is a trademark of The Globe Pequot Press, Inc.

Library of Congress Cataloging-in-Publication Data
Hoffman, James L. (James Lawrence), 1963–.
    Family Adventure Guide : North Carolina/ by James L. Hoffman. — 1st ed.
        p.   cm. — (Family adventure guide series)
    "A voyager book."
    Includes indexes.
    ISBN 1-56440-751-9
    1. North Carolina—Guide Books. 2. Family recreation—North Carolina—
Guidebooks. I. Title. II. Series.
F252.3.H64   1996
917.5604'43—dc20   96–16737
                                                            CIP

Manufactured in the United States of America
First Edition/Second Printing

For Daphne, Mike, and Jess
I cherish you

ACKNOWLEDGMENTS

I would like to thank the following for their help in writing this book: Daphne Hoffman, K. R. and Patricia Hoffman, Sara Pitzer, Dana Teague, the North Carolina Division of Travel and Tourism, and all the other people across the state, including park rangers, museum guides, tourism officials from various cities and counties, and others who provided the details for this guide.

NORTH CAROLINA

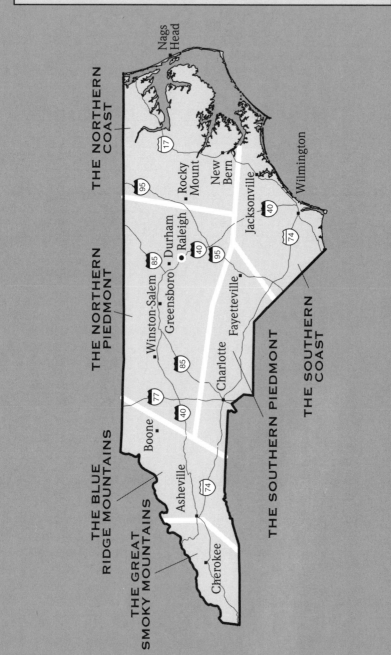

Nags
Head

17

95

Rocky
Mount

New
Bern

Wilmington

85

Durham

Raleigh

40

95

Jacksonville

40

74

THE NORTHERN
COAST

Winston-Salem

Greensboro

Fayetteville

THE NORTHERN
PIEDMONT

85

Charlotte

THE SOUTHERN
COAST

77

40

THE SOUTHERN PIEDMONT

Boone

74

Asheville

THE BLUE
RIDGE MOUNTAINS

Cherokee

THE GREAT
SMOKY MOUNTAINS

CONTENTS

INTRODUCTION

I t seems to me that living in North Carolina is a privilege. My family and I are particularly lucky because we live in the Piedmont, where you can easily reach the mountains, the beaches, or the state's larger cities for travel and entertainment. I have many fond memories of my life here as a child, as a college student, and as an adult with my own family. We've been pretty much everywhere in the Tarheel state, from Murphy to Manteo, as the expression goes. We've enjoyed the majesty of the mountains and the history and beauty of the coast. But one interesting thing occurred in the process of writing this book. I would ask the kids if they remembered going to the Indian village in the mountains or the loggerhead turtle that nested in front of the rental beach house, and almost every time the response would be a puzzled "NO." That could be due to their young ages or it could be a clever ploy to get me to take them back to these places. Oh well, I guess we'll have to do it all again.

I've divided the state into six travel areas that roughly resemble the state's geographic regions. We begin our journey in the west in the Great Smoky Mountains and continue through the Blue Ridge Mountains, both part of the Appalachian Range. Next, we go to the Northern Piedmont, traveling from west to east, and then back to the Southern Piedmont, where we again travel from west to east. Finally, we move into the coastal plain, which I've divided into the Southern Coast and the Northern Coast.

Each chapter is organized geographically, so you can use this guide to easily plan your itinerary or to find an adventure near you by flipping backward or forward a page or two. In addition, you'll find two indexes —one general and one by type of activity—to help you select appropriate attractions and events for your family.

You'll also find listed throughout the book my recommendations for these attractions and events. In addition, we've included reference maps to help get you on the road. I wrote this book with the help of the map created by the North Carolina Department of Transportation, which is distributed free of charge. You can obtain a copy of it and more information by calling (919) 733–7600, or (800) 847–4848 if you are outside North Carolina.

One more thing: Have a great time exploring the great state of North Carolina!

The prices and rates listed in this guidebook were confirmed at press time. We recommend, however, that you call establishments to obtain current information before traveling.

FAMILY ADVENTURE GUIDE™

NORTH CAROLINA

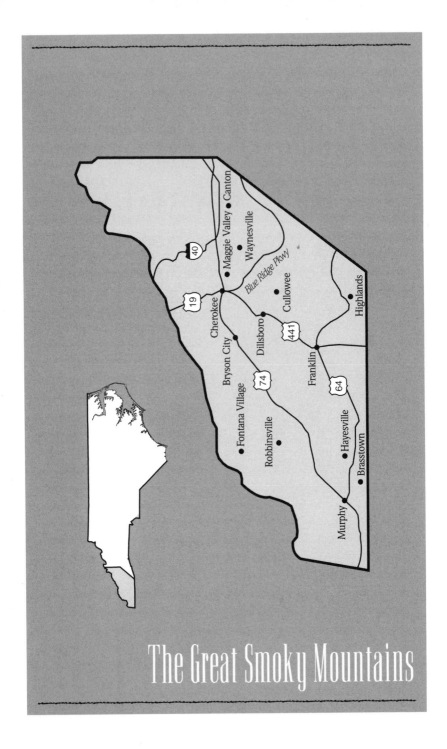

The Great Smoky Mountains

The Great Smoky Mountains

The Great Smoky Mountains are just south of heaven. You'll find that the beauty of the area is unmatched as you climb to heights of more than 6,000 feet—some of the highest points in the eastern United States. The region includes the most popular national park in the country as well as one of the last virgin wildernesses. The trout fishing is great, too. Hiking trails, gorgeous flowing waterfalls, and crystal-like streams are waiting around just about every corner.

In this region you can take a wild rafting adventure down one of a number of rivers, mine precious stones, ride an old-fashioned railway, or visit a theme park. The heritage of the area is as important here as it is anywhere. You can visit a Cherokee Indian reservation or learn about the Europeans who settled in this area. And don't miss all the country food and crafts the Great Smoky Mountains have to offer.

Travel is generally slow in this area, as it is over most of the mountains of North Carolina. Don't try to take in too much at one time, or you'll spend all your time driving and miss all the fun. U.S. Highway 64 runs through the southern portion of the state and is your best bet for long travel. U.S. Highway 74 runs from the northeast portion of the region to intersect with Highway 64. It combines with several other highways along the way, so don't let that confuse you. Highway 441 bisects the area and runs north to south. Smoky Mountain Host, a visitors center based in Franklin, can assist you with general information on the region. Call them at (800) 432–4678.

MURPHY

Nestled in the westernmost corner of North Carolina is Cherokee County. First settled by the Cherokee Indians, it offers an abundance of opportunities for outdoor activities. The **Hanging Dog Recreation Area,** located on Hiwassee Lake just 5 miles northwest of Murphy, offers a large campground, a picnic area, an opportunity for swimming, and hiking trails. Only small trailers are allowed at the campground. Contact Nantahala National Forest at (704) 257–4200 for more information.

Learn about the Cherokee Indians' presence here and about early American life at the **Cherokee County Historical Museum,** located at 205 Peachtree Street in downtown Murphy. The museum features an extensive collection of more than 2,000 Indian artifacts and exhibits on early mountain life. You'll see tools and housewares that have been used throughout the years, in addition to displays that explain the Trail of Tears —a forced westward march of more than 70,000 Native Americans following the U.S. Congress's 1830 passage of the Indian Removal Act—and the suffering of the Cherokee Indian Nation. Admission is free. The museum is open from 9:00 A.M. to noon and 1:00 to 5:00 P.M. Monday through Friday. Call (704) 837–6792 for more information.

The county's most unique attraction is a biblical theme park, covering 200 acres of mountainside. You won't find any flashy rides or games at the **Fields of the Wood,** located on Highway 294 southwest of Murphy. This very different park features the Ten Commandments displayed in stone on one of those mountainsides and the world's largest cross and altar. You can also see a depiction of Christ's tomb and displays on biblical teachings. You'll want to visit the park's Bible, book, and gift shop as well. Admission to the park is free and it's open daily, generally from sunrise to sunset. Call (704) 494–7855 for more information.

BRASSTOWN

Located east of Murphy, just south off Highway 64, is Brasstown and the **John C. Campbell Folk School.** The 365-acre campus is home to what is recognized as the nation's only instructional folk program. The school, founded in 1925, has become a real asset to the small community and is listed in the National Register of Historic Places.

A variety of special events, celebrations, and presentations are held throughout the year. The biggest, the Fall Festival, is held the first weekend in October and features crafts, music, and more. You can visit many of the campus buildings anytime and perhaps see one of the famous Brasstown carvers at work. The small museum of crafts in the log cabin, the sawmill, and the millhouse are also open to the public. In addition, the school offers minicourses lasting from two days to two weeks in blacksmithing, wood working, pottery, wood carving, weaving, basketry, mountain music, folk dancing, gardening, jewelry making, and folklore. Most short courses are offered on weekends. Admission to the campus is free, but a fee is charged for many of the special events and instructional programs. Call (800) 365–5724 for more information.

HAYESVILLE

Travel just a couple more miles east on Highway 64 and exit to the north. Here you'll find Hayesville and a chance to get out on the lake. **Lake Chatuge,** which straddles the North Carolina–Georgia state line, offers facilities for camping, fishing, swimming, and picnicking. In addition, you'll find hiking trails, boat rentals, and a visitor center. At **Jackrabbit Mountain** recreation area off State Road 1155, you'll find facilities for trailers up to 22 feet long. If the sites are full at Jackrabbit, another nice campground is less than 30 miles east. **Standing Indian Mountain,** located just off Highway 64, offers remarkable trout fishing, hiking trails, and scenic drives around the area. The park has become popular for mountain biking enthusiasts, and both wilderness and developed camping sites are offered. Overnight camping at both recreation areas is $8.00 per night. Jackrabbit is open May through September, Standing Indian Mountain is open April through November. For more information on either recreation area, contact the Nantahala National Forest at (704) 257–4200.

While you're in or near Hayesville, you might want to check out the **Peacock Playhouse,** where the Licklog Players present productions throughout the year. Licklog Players is a volunteer organization, but the group produces professional-quality performances ranging from drama to musicals to comedy. The theater seats about 250 people for the shows, and the annual playbill always includes some family-oriented productions. Ticket

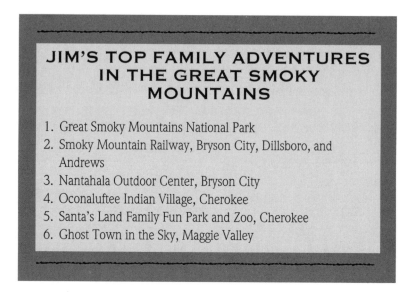

JIM'S TOP FAMILY ADVENTURES
IN THE GREAT SMOKY
MOUNTAINS

1. Great Smoky Mountains National Park
2. Smoky Mountain Railway, Bryson City, Dillsboro, and
   Andrews
3. Nantahala Outdoor Center, Bryson City
4. Oconaluftee Indian Village, Cherokee
5. Santa's Land Family Fun Park and Zoo, Cherokee
6. Ghost Town in the Sky, Maggie Valley

prices start at $9.00 for adults and $6.00 for children and students. Call
(704) 389–8632 for more information, directions, or to make reservations.

Nearby you'll find **Tusquittee Campground and Cabins,** which
provides the perfect opportunity to head to the great outdoors, particularly
for families with young children or family members who don't want to
camp in a tent. The park, located on Tusquittee Road just east of
Hayesville, provides full-service log cabins, creekside camper cabins for
more rustic living, and traditional trailer and tent camping sites. The campground also has a heated bathhouse, hiking trails, a swimming hole, a
swing set, and equipment for badminton, teatherball, volleyball, and horseshoes. Rates for campsites start at $10 per night, and cabin rental starts at
$25 per night. The campground is open from April through November.
Call (704) 389–8520 for more information or to make reservations.

FRANKLIN

Continuing east on Highway 64 and heading north on State Highway 28
brings you to the town of Franklin, seat of Macon County. In addition to
the logging industry, tourism has become very important to the Franklin

area economy. While accommodations—cottages, cabins, chalets, and vacation homes—fill the area, its natural beauty is still undisturbed. The Franklin Area Chamber of Commerce (704-524-3161) can provide information on accommodations.

The biggest attractions for tourists are the mines, where you can hunt for and retrieve genuine rubies, sapphires, and other native stones—plus precious stones sometimes imported to make the hunting more interesting. There are a dozen mining operations open to tourists in the area. Some require digging, while others confine your gem hunting to a flume. You'll want to call ahead to find out if equipment is included in the mining fee. Fees charged by each of the mines vary. Some charge $1.00 to $3.00 per bucket, while others have an $8.00 to $12.00 admission fee and then charge a nominal per-bucket fee. Most are open during daylight hours, and you can find one open any day of the week. Most mines are open April through October. Here's a list of them, their general locations, and their phone numbers:

Gem City Mine, located north on Highway 441, (704) 524–3967; **Gold City Gem Mine,** located on Highway 441/23, (704) 369–3905; **Jackson Hole,** located on Highway 64, (704) 524–5850; **Jacobs Ruby Mine,** Ruby Mine Road, (704) 524–7022; **Jones Ruby Mine,** 52 Lloyd Tallent Road, (704) 524–5946; **Mason Mountain Mine,** 895 Bryson City Road, (704) 524–4570; **Mason's Ruby and Sapphire Mine,** 85 Upper Burningtown Road, (704) 369–9742; **Moonstone Gem Mine,** located on Lower Burningtown Road, (704) 524–7764; **Rocky Face Gem Mine,** 30 Sanderstown Road, (704) 524–3148; **Rose Creek Mine & Campground,** 28 Lyle Downs Road, (704) 524–3225; **Sheffield Mine,** 160 Leatherman Gap Road, (704) 369–8383; **Shuler Ruby Mine,** 245 Ruby Mine Road, (704) 524–3551; **The Old Cardinal Gem Mine,** 22 Mason Branch Road, (704) 369–7534.

If you don't have much luck hunting for gems on your own, stop by one of the many shops in the area or at the **Franklin Gem and Mineral Museum,** 2 West Main Street, in the old jail. The museum, operated by the Franklin Gem and Mineral Society, features displays of all the native stones and a little bit about the history of the area's development. Admission is free. The museum is open from May 1 to October 31, from 10:00

A.M. to 4:00 P.M. Monday through Saturday and 1:00 to 4:00 P.M. Sunday. Call (704) 369–7831 for more information.

Another museum here takes you to Scotland. The **Scottish Tartans Museum and Heritage Center,** 33 East Main Street in downtown Franklin, is an extension of the Scottish Tartans Society. The museum includes displays on the tartan and Highland dress from as far back as 1700, as well as the evolution of the kilt. A research library also provides information on the Scottish influence on the Appalachian and Cherokee cultures. If you have a Scottish background, you can try to find your roots. Admission is free. The museum is open from May through October, from 10:00 A.M. to 5:00 P.M. Tuesday through Saturday and 1:00 to 5:00 P.M. Sunday. From November through April it's open from 10:00 A.M. to 5:00 P.M. Wednesday through Saturday. Call (704) 524–7472 for more information.

During your stay in Franklin, a ride east on Highway 64 is a must. The best idea is to bring along a picnic lunch, and don't forget the camera for a scenic drive to **Highlands,** the second highest incorporated town in the eastern United States. The drive on this byway takes about 20 minutes and is truly lovely. It ends at Highlands, where you'll find two of the most photographed waterfalls in the area. Headed east, you first come to **Dry Falls** about 2 miles before you get to Highlands. From the parking lot an easy paved trail will take you behind, actually underneath, the 75-foot falls. Next, about 1 mile down the road, you come to **Bridal Veil Falls.** Here you can drive behind the 120-foot falls, which you'll first see from the highway. You should be able to tell how this thin veil of running water got its name. On the other side of the highway, about 2 miles back to the west, are a campground and a picnic area. **Cliffside Lake & Van Hook Glade** offers a picnic, camping, swimming, fishing, and hiking facilities. You can call the Highlands Ranger at (704) 526–3765 if you need more information or assistance while in this area.

To complete this scenic drive (a total of 61 miles), you'll have to backtrack to Franklin—that's west on Highway 64—to State Road 1310, also referred to as Wayah Road. Your drive takes you along Wayah Creek, which is mostly private, to **Wayah Bald**—the county's highest peak at 5,345 feet. In this area you can hike part of the Appalachian Trail, have a picnic, see wildlife, and learn about how the natural beauty has been pre-served despite more than a century of development. Take Forest Road 69, a 1-mile gravel road not on state maps, to see the **Wilson Lick Ranger Station.** Built in 1913, it was the first ranger station in Nantahala National Forest. If you go three more miles up the road, you can park and take the paved trail to **Wayah Bald Fire Tower.** This tower, built by the Civilian Conservation Corps in the 1930s, provides a breathtaking view of the mountains of the Carolinas, as well as those of northern Georgia and Ten-nessee. A picnic area and two more hiking trails are located nearby. You might want to check in with the Wayah Rangers District (704–524–6441) before you head out on these trails. Some are more difficult than others.

Your next destination should be **Nantahala Lake,** about 6 miles west of Wayah Bald. With about 29 miles of shoreline, this lake offers fish-ing and boating. Picnic facilities are available on either side of the lake, accessible via State Road 1310. Nantahala River feeds the lake and pro-vides excellent trout fishing, but you'll have to obtain the proper license. If you live outside North Carolina or you don't fish much, you can get a license to fish for one or three days. Most tackle stores can sell you the license best suited for your needs. Temporary licenses cost $5.00 per day for residents, $10.00 per day or $15.00 for three days for non-residents. State Road 1310 ends at Highway 19, near Andrews. Here you can finish your day trip and stop for a while to watch experienced water enthusiasts rafting, canoeing, and kayaking. A walkway gives you an excellent view of the ride over Nantahala Falls.

ROBBINSVILLE

Northwest of Nantahala Lake at the intersection of U.S. Highway 129 and State Highway 143 is the town of Robbinsville. It lies at the eastern edge of one of the most impressive, undisturbed wilderness areas you will find in the country. Dedicated in 1936 to the poet who wrote *Trees*, the **Joyce Kilmer Memorial Forest** is truly a site to behold. Some of the trees in the forest are hundreds of years old, stand more than 100 feet high, and are 20 feet in diameter at the base. Here you will see a wide variety of trees, including yellow poplar, hemlock, sycamore, basswood, dogwood, beech, and oak, that burst into a blaze of red, yellow, and orange in early October.

In spring, wildflowers, rhododendrons, mountain laurels, and azaleas take over the 3,800 acres, but you can't take the beauty with you when you go; removing any vegetation is prohibited by law. Let your camera capture your souvenirs.

The forest is part of the 14,000-acre **Slickrock Wilderness Area,** where you'll find more than 60 miles of hiking trails that run along ridges and beside cool mountain streams. A picnic area is located on Route 416 at the entrance. You can call the ranger's office at (704) 479–6431 for more information. To camp close to the site, you probably want to head to **Horse Cove Campground,** located northwest of Robbinsville near the Slickrock Wilderness Area. In addition, **Cheoah Point Campground,** located on Santeetlah Lake off Highway 129, offers a host of recreational activities. Campsites cost $5.00 per night. Horse Cove is open year-round, but Cheoah Point closes between October and April. For more information, contact the Nantahala National Forest office at (704) 257–4200.

FONTANA VILLAGE

Fontana Village Resort, located north of Robbinsville along Highway 28, is the largest established resort in the area. Built by the Tennessee Valley Authority (TVA) in the early 1940s to house construction workers who were building **Fontana Dam,** the town was turned into a family resort following World War II. Today, it has maintained its rustic, historic charm but offers everything you need for a wonderful, relaxing vacation.

While you visit here, you'll want to see Fontana Dam, an elaborate engineering feat for the time. Not only is the dam impressive, so is the fact that the TVA built a railroad and an entire community—including a hospital, bank, library, post office, and schools—essentially overnight. Fontana Dam is a massive concrete structure that stands 480 feet above its rock foundation, creating a 10,600-acre lake. From the visitor center at the top of the dam, you can take a tram or cable car into the powerhouse, where you'll see educational displays on the production of hydroelectricity. There is no admission charge. The visitor center is open from 9:00 A.M. to 8:00 P.M. daily, May through October.

Fontana Village Resort offers 94 rooms at **Fontana Inn** as well as 200 cottages. The cottages, ranging from one to three bedrooms, come with all cooking and eating utensils. Rates for a family range from $79 per day at the inn to $109 per day at a cottage. **Fontana Campground,** located on the Little Tennessee River near the dam, offers tent and trailer camping sites. You'll find something for everyone in the family at this self-contained resort. There are three swimming pools, including one indoor pool, and a number of hot tubs that you can enjoy year-round. The kids will certainly love the village's nearby waterslide. A crafts workshop (with gift shop) provides instruction in copper tooling, enameling, basketry, leather crafting, and stenciling. The kids might like the opportunity to learn the craft of shirt painting or how to build a bird house. An activities center provides equipment for bike riding, archery, badminton, tennis, volleyball, shuffleboard, and horseshoes. The recreation department also plans structured activities such as softball and basketball games, pony rides, and guided hikes and bike rides. For information on Fontana Village attractions, call (800) 849–2258.

Finding a place to eat won't be a problem at Fontana Village. You will probably want to try **Peppermill Cafeteria** more than once if you're staying for any length of time. The cafeteria is definitely family oriented and offers a hearty selection of mountain country cuisine.

Great Smoky Mountain Stables, located in Fontana Village, offers pony rides for children under the age of ten at a cost of $5.00 for ten minutes. For older children and adults, rides on trails through the dense forests of the area are offered at a cost of $10.00 per half hour. Call (704) 498–2211 for more information.

You can take a self-guided tour to the **Log Cabin Museum,** built in 1875. Here you'll see many of the tools and relics that tell the history of the area's development. You'll learn about the Trail of Tears and the removal of the Cherokee people and the arrival of the logging industry. The cabin is located in the heart of the village. Hours vary and are irregular.

Fontana Marina, located about $1\frac{1}{2}$ miles from the village on Fontana Lake, offers boat and equipment rentals, water sports equipment, and fishing tips. Prices on boat rentals range from $8.00 per hour or $20.00 per day for a fishing boat with no motor to a nineteen-person pontoon boat that rents for $75.00 per hour or $525.00 per day. Fishing licenses are available here as well.

If you want to get out on the water but prefer letting someone else do the work, try one of the two cruises the marina offers during the day. You can take a picnic cruise at noon for $14.00 per person or a sight-seeing cruise at 2:00 P.M. for $7.00 per person. At 9:30 A.M. and 3:00 P.M., you can ride down the lake to the location where the 1994 motion picture *Nell*, starring Jodie Foster, was filmed. The cost is $10.00 per adult and $5.00 per child age nine or younger.

The U.S. Forest Service operates two campgrounds in the Fontana Village area. **Tsali Trail and Camping Area,** located off Highway 28, has forty-one campsites and offers rest rooms and showers. Here you can hike, bike, and enjoy all the fun the lake has to offer. The cost is $10 per site per night. **Cable Cove,** located just east on Highway 28, is a smaller recreation area and costs $5.00 per site per night. Both campgrounds are open April through October. For more information, contact the Nantahala National Forest office at (704) 257–4200.

BRYSON CITY

Bryson City, east of Fontana Village and accessible off Highway 74, is an outdoor recreation center for the area and one of two North Carolina entrances to the **Great Smoky Mountains National Park**. Fontana Lake forms the southwestern border of the park, which covers a total of 520,000 acres and is bisected by the North Carolina–Tennessee state line. This is the most-visited national park in the United States, but don't worry if you're looking for space to stretch out. You'll find plenty of room to fish, hike, and camp. The mountains of the park are among the oldest in the world and rise more than 6,000 feet. Plant and animal life is varied, with more than 130 species of trees identified in the park. In the spring, the park comes alive with color as azaleas and wildflowers begin to bloom. Among the animal life that you might spot in the park are deer, wild turkey, ruffed grouse, and bear. You'll also find 900 miles of horseback riding and hiking trails and 735 miles of fishing streams. Many area campgrounds have organized activities, including presentations by park rangers and by people from the Cherokee Indian Reservation. You can contact the Great Smoky Mountains National Park office at (615) 436–1200 for more information on the park and its campgrounds.

Make sure you take a drive up **The Road to Nowhere** from Bryson City to the national park. It was meant to be a route from Bryson City to Fontana Village when construction was begun following World War II. Bits and pieces of the road were built until the 1960s to the east side of Fontana Lake. Now it's one of the prettiest drives in the park.

One of the best ways to see the area is by taking a ride on the **Great Smoky Mountain Railway.** The railway offers regularly scheduled trips from April through December, originating in Bryson City, Dillsboro to the south, and Andrews to the west, on a train pulled by a steam locomotive or one of four conventional diesel locomotives. While there are a number of different trips offered, the most popular is a four-hour excursion along Fontana Lake to the Nantahala Gorge and back. Beverages and snacks are available on the trains, and you can ride either in a comfortable enclosed coach or in an open car, which provides breathtaking views and excellent photo opportunities. Railway trips start at $16.00 for adults and $7.00 for children age twelve or younger. Call (800) 872–4681 for more information.

Experience the excitement of the white water with any number of outfitters along North Carolina's rivers. (Courtesy Nantahala Outdoor Center)

Perhaps the most popular activity in the area is rafting, and you can combine the railway trip with a white-water rafting trip. Two of the largest rafting outfitters, **Wildwater, Ltd.** (800–451–9972) and the **Nantahala Outdoor Center** (800–232–7238), offer special packages in conjunction with the railway. The area has several rivers that accommodate adventure seekers ready to get out on the water, but the Nantahala is by far the most popular. While some rivers may be too dangerous for a family excursion, the Nantahala is considered safe for children. Most outfitters will allow children as young as seven (a minimum of 60 pounds) on the trips. You'll see eight other outfitters scattered along the river, and you may want to check with several to find a trip that suits your needs. Admission for rafting excursions starts at around $10. The cost of the seven-hour raft and rail excursion starts at $48 for adults, $37 for children twelve and younger, free for children under two, and includes a picnic lunch. The Swain County Chamber of Commerce can provide you with information on the rafting companies as well as information on lodging and private camp-grounds in the Bryson City area. Call them at (800) 867–9246.

CHEROKEE

Just a few miles east of Bryson City on Highway 19 is the town of Chero-kee and the **Cherokee Indian Reservation,** offering a chance to go back in time and see how these people have lived for thousands of years. Cherokee is the sole town located in the 56,000-acre Qualla Boundary Cherokee Indian Reservation, which is home to roughly 8,500 members of the Eastern Band of the Cherokee. It is nestled between the Great Smoky Mountains National Park and the western end of the Blue Ridge Parkway. You can get a complete listing of accommodations in this area by calling (800) 438–1601.

You'll want to take a lot of time to explore this area, and the best place to begin is at the **Museum of the Cherokee Indian,** located at Highway 441 and Drama Road. The museum gives you an introduction to the Chero-kee heritage, history, and culture. In front is a 20-foot California Redwood statue of Sequoyah, who invented the Cherokee alphabet. In addition to a big collection of clothes, crafts, weapons, and artifacts—some of which are more than 10,000 years old—the museum also has an art gallery and theaters

Crafts, such as baskets, are still made the old-fashioned way at Oconaluftee Indian Village. (Courtesy the Cherokee Tribal Promotion Office)

where you can learn about this culture's history in audio-visual shows. Especially interesting are special phones allowing you to hear the Cherokee language spoken. Admission is $4.00 for adults and $2.00 for children ages six through twelve. From May to mid-June, the museum is open from 9:00 A.M. to 6:00 P.M. Monday through Saturday and 9:00 A.M. to 6:00 P.M. Sunday. From mid-June through August, the museum is open from 9:00 A.M. to 8:00 P.M. Monday through Saturday and 9:00 A.M. to 5:00 P.M. Sunday. Call (704) 497–3481 for more information.

While you will see a number of people dressed in Indian attire, complete with headdress and ready to be photographed, these are not authentically dressed Cherokee. The real way the Indians lived can be seen at several attractions on the reservation. One of the most enlightening places to visit in the Cherokee area is the **Oconaluftee Indian Village,** where the past comes alive. The village, located just off Highway 441, is an authentic re-creation of an eighteenth-century Cherokee Indian community. Here costumed guides will take you on a tour of the village, where you will see local people working at the ancient arts of basket making, pottery, and finger weaving, an art that involves using the fingers in place of a shuttle to produce colorful belts, headbands, and other articles. You can also visit the seven-sided council house—a wood and dirt structure—and learn how the Cherokee tribes functioned. Admission is $8.00 for adults and $4.00 for children ages six through twelve. From mid-May to late October, the village is open from 9:00 A.M. to 5:30 P.M. daily. Call (704) 497–2111 for more information.

Located near the village is the Cherokees' **Mountainside Theater,** where *Unto These Hills* is performed during the summer. The outdoor drama, written by Kermit Hunter, is an inspirational piece that captures the history of the Cherokee Indian from the mid-1500s and leads to the tragedy of the Trail of Tears in the late 1830s. The Cherokee people originally settled much of this land, but many were forced off it by the U.S. government and made to march to Arkansas and Oklahoma. During these marches more than 4,000 of the 15,000 Indians involved died of disease or exposure. Others, whose ancestors still live here, managed to escape into the mountains. The play, produced by more than 130 performers and technicians, runs about two hours. Tickets for reserved seats cost $11.00 per person, all ages.

General-admission tickets cost $9.00 for adults and $5.00 for children through age twelve. Shows are presented at 8:00 P.M. Monday through Saturday from mid-June through late August. Call (704) 497–2111 for more information or to make reservations.

You can celebrate Christmas during the summer at **Santa's Land Family Fun Park and Zoo.** An especially good attraction for younger children, it is located on Highway 19, a few minutes' drive east of Cherokee. The kids can talk to Santa and his elves and visit the animals in the petting zoo, where they will see dozens of domestic and exotic animals. You'll also find paddle boats, train rides, and the Rudi-Coaster. Admission to this winter wonderland is $11.95 for children and adults. Children two and under are admitted free. The admission includes all rides, entertainment, and exhibits. The park is open from May through October. Hours are 9:00 A.M. to 5:00 P.M. daily. For more information call (704) 497–9191.

More modern recreation is waiting at **Cherokee Fun Park,** located on Highway 441 near the entrance to the Great Smoky Mountains National Park. The park features four acres of go-carts, bumper boats, miniature golf, and a big game room. Admission is charged for each attraction, and hours vary according to season and weather. Rides for adults and older children, such as bumper boats and go-carts, cost $4.00 per ride; rides in the kiddy park cost $1.50. Miniature golf is $3.50 per person. Call (704) 497–5877 for more information.

You don't want to forget about all the outdoor activities the Cherokee area has to offer. Trout fishing on the Cherokee Indian reservation is excellent, and you'll find hundreds of miles of streams and several ponds in the area. Two North Carolina trout fishing records have been established on the reservation in recent years. A special reservation fishing license costs $5.00 per day, and children younger than twelve can fish on a parent's license.

Whether you want to stay in a luxury hotel, a cabin, or at a campground, you won't have any problem finding a place to suit your recreational needs. One of the best campgrounds nearby is **Smokemont Campground,** 6 miles north of Cherokee off Highway 441 in the Smokemont community. In addition to fishing streams and hiking trails, you'll also find great horseback riding trails and stables where you can make arrangements to rent horses. Smokemont Campground is open year-round, and sites cost $11. **Deep Creek Campground,** located west of Cherokee back toward Bryson City, off Highway 19, is another good place to set up housekeeping in the woods. In addition to traditional campground activities, such as hiking and fishing, this park offers a chance for a leisurely cruise down the creek in an inner tube. Many of the businesses located nearby will rent you an inner tube for less than $5.00 a day.

KOA Kampgrounds, located on Star Route north of Cherokee is the largest commercial campground in the area. It offers a wide range of sites, from primitive tent sites to paved sites with full hookups to rustic cabins on the creek, that fit any budget. You will also find a wide variety of activities at the 35-acre campground, including swimming, tennis, volleyball, a game room, and more. The campground's Fun Bus is also ready to take you on a fun-filled day trip or shuttle you up the river for a 3-mile tubing trip. Call (704) 497–9711 for more information.

MAGGIE VALLEY

Keep heading east on Highway 19 and you'll be in Maggie Valley. **Ghost Town in the Sky,** a great western theme park, should be first on your family's itinerary on a trip to this area. Here you can relive the adventures of frontier life against a beautiful mountain backdrop. You enter the park up a steep, 3,300-foot mountainside by an inclined railway or chairlift (a shuttle bus is available for the queasy). Stay alert as you browse through the Old West shops and displays because, just as in the frontier days, you never know when you'll be in the middle of a "gunfight" or "bank robbery." The park includes more than thirty rides and shows, including a roller coaster that almost casts you out over a mile-high mountainside. You can enjoy music and dancing at the old city hall or belly up to the bar at the Silver Dollar Saloon for the honky-tonk piano and can-can dancers. Country music abounds, and shows are presented continuously at the Mile High Fun Center. Snacks, as well as full meals and picnic facilities, are available at Ghost Town. Admission is about $15 for adults and around $10 for children ages three through nine. The park is open the first Saturday in May through the last Sunday in October, from 9:00 A.M. to 6:00 P.M. daily. Call (704) 926–1140 for more information.

You can plan to spend several hours in downtown Maggie Valley, its streets lined with specialty shops, restaurants, and various amusements. The community is a popular tourist resort and gets crowded during peak vacation times, but that doesn't spoil the old-time country feel of the town. Accommodations are as varied here as they are throughout the Smoky Mountains, but the best thing about this area's hotels and cottages is the spectacular view of the landscape that many of them offer. The Maggie Valley Area Chamber of Commerce (800–624–4431) can provide you with information on accommodations in the area.

Some standard family tourist attractions are also located near the center of town. The **Mini-Apolis Entertainment Center,** 250 Soco Road, offers five racing tracks, bumper boats, a small gem mine, a game room, and miniature golf. The girls in the family (both big and small) may get a kick out of a visit to the doll and gift shop. Admission of $3.00 to $5.00 is charged for each attraction. Call (704) 926–1685 for more information. If it's raining, spend an afternoon at the **Red Barn Miniature Golf,** located on Highway 19/276, outside Maggie Valley. This indoor golf course and arcade could be the right solution to your rainy-day needs. Golf costs $2.50 per person, and children younger than three get a free game. Call (704) 926–1901 for more information.

Soco Gardens Zoo, located just down Soco Road, features a small collection of mammals, reptiles, and birds from around the country. The zoo is very clean and well kept. Even if it rains, you can still enjoy a walk through the zoo on covered walkways. The kids certainly will want to visit the petting zoo. The zoo is open in May, September, and October from 10:00 A.M. to 6:00 P.M. daily. From June through August, it's open from 9:00 A.M. to dusk. Admission is $4.75 for adults and $2.75 for children ages five through twelve. Call (704) 926–1746 for more information

Get out your dancing shoes when you visit **The Stompin' Ground,** located near the zoo. Here you get a glimpse of mountain heritage through clogging and mountain dancing adapted from the area's Irish and Scottish heritage. You'll be moved to stomp your feet yourself during the show presented nightly. Admission to the shows is $7.00 for adults and $3.00 for children three to twelve years of age. Shows begin at 8:00 P.M. Call (704) 926–1288 for more information.

To get out of the crowds, give **Cataloochee Ranch** a try. Located

JIM'S TOP ANNUAL EVENTS IN THE GREAT SMOKY MOUNTAINS

Riverfest, late May, Bryson City, (704) 488–6159

Folkmoot-USA, late July, Waynesville area, (704) 648–2730

Mountain Heritage Day, September, Cullowhee, (704) 227–7129

Mountain Life Festival, mid-September, Cherokee, (704) 497–9146

John C. Campbell Folkschool Fall Festival, early October, Brasstown, (800) 365–5724

just a few miles north of Maggie Valley, the resort has been operating for more than sixty years. Here you not only find the aura of a rugged sheep and cattle farm, but you can also enjoy all the amenities of a modern vacation. The 1,000-acre ranch is one of only three private entrances to the Great Smoky Mountains National Park. The ranch offers individual cabins as well rooms at the Silverbell Lodge and at the ranch house. The vegetable garden produces a great variety of food that you'll find makes its way to your dinner table in a family-style setting. In addition to meals, the only structured activity at the ranch is horseback riding. The rest of the time is your own, as the lodge offers tennis, hiking, trout fishing, horseshoes, table tennis, badminton, and croquet. You can relax by the swimming pool, take a hayride, or walk through the ranch's glorious meadows, where wildflowers abound in spring and summer. Rates at the ranch house start at $120 per night and cabins start at $180 per night. Two meals a day are included. The rates also allow you to enjoy all the recreational facilities at the ranch except horseback riding. Those trips start at $30 for a half day. Call (800) 868–1401 for more information.

Perhaps the best thing about the ranch is that it's right next door to the **Cataloochee Ski Area,** With the help of snow makers, the North Carolina ski season usually starts in early December. Cataloochee has nine slopes and trails that range from gentle slopes for beginners to the monstrous 5,400-foot Moody Top. Rates for lift tickets on a weekday start at $14 per adult for a half day, $13 per student for a half day, and $10 per child, ages seven through twelve. Full-day lift tickets start at $20 for adults, $16 for students, and $13 for children. Equipment rental starts at $10 for adults and $9 for students and children. The Cataloochee Ski School offers lessons, starting at $12 for a one-and-a-half-hour session. Call (800) 768–0285 for more information. Inquire about special lesson packages for children and family special days. Hours of operation may vary according to weather.

WAYNESVILLE

Highway 19 to Highway 23 will take you to Waynesville, a small, quaint mountain community that still has brick sidewalks in the downtown district. Here you'll find more than 100 charming shops, galleries, and restaurants. Among them you find the **Candy Barrel** (704–452–0075) and **Smith's Drugs** (704–456–0607), where you can get a drink from the old-fashioned soda fountain. Everything from antiques to clothes is available in the shopping district, but you might want to schedule your trip here for late July. Waynesville is home to **Folkmoot-USA,** an annual international festival that brings 300 dancers and musicians from around the world. The event is usually held the last weekend in July and begins with a parade on Friday afternoon on Main Street. On Saturday, musicians and dancers perform and mingle with guests. More than 100 booths feature gifts, crafts, and food from around the world.

While you are in Waynesville stop in at the **Museum of North Carolina Handicrafts,** 307 Shelton Street. Housed in the Shelton House, a farm home built in 1875, the museum features works by some of the state's best-known artisans. Here you'll see hand-carved dulcimers, unique carved bowls, and items children will love like wooden, mule-drawn wagons and sleds. The Indian room features a collection of Navajo rugs, baskets, and jewelry as well as Cherokee crafts and artifacts. Admission is free and hours vary. Call (704) 452–1551 for more information.

CANTON

The **Canton Area Historical Museum,** located on Park Street in Canton, just a few miles west of Waynesville, is a small but interesting museum. It offers a look at how this area, once a hunting and fishing ground for the Cherokee Indians, was developed. Following European settlement, it became a popular stopping point for western ranchers moving their cattle and swine to market in the east. In addition, the Pigeon River made it an important shipping point, leading to the establishment of the Champion Paper Mill, which remains the area's biggest employer. This history is presented in displays of the mill and with area artifacts, pictures, and records that provide a glimpse into life from the late 1800s to the present. Admission is free. Museum hours are 10:00 A.M. to noon and 1:00 to 4:00 P.M. Monday through Friday and 2:00 to 4:00 P.M. Sunday. Call (704) 646–3412 for more information.

DILLSBORO

Dillsboro, located at the junction of highways 23/441 and 74, is a small historic community and one of three area towns where you can catch a ride on the Great Smoky Mountain Railway (see Bryson City entry for more information on the railway). Located next to the depot is the **Historic Railway Museum.** Here you will see more than 3,000 articles of railroad memorabilia that carry you back more than 140 years. The kids will enjoy seeing the scale models of trains and railways. Video booths offer four features: "The Making of *The Fugitive,*" which is about the movie starring Harrison Ford that was filmed in the area; "Riding on Steam Engine #1702"; "History of the Railroad"; and "The Railway and the Community." Admission is $3.00 for adults and $2.00 for children two to twelve years of age. Hours vary according to the annual railway schedule. Call (704) 586–8811 for more information.

Maintaining the distinction of an old railway town, Dillsboro has been turned into a charming shopping and historic district. The **Dillsboro Historic District** is nestled at the edges of the Great Smoky Mountains on the Tuckasegee River. Log cabins and homes from the late 1800s provide showcases for handmade crafts and homemade treats. You can get a walking map of the district by calling the Jackson County Visitor's Center at

(800) 962–1911. Then just park your car and stroll through the village, where you find very friendly shopkeepers and artisans. The kids might find the perfect gift for Mom at the **Apron Shop** (704–586–9391), which also offers hand-crafted pillows and quilts. For the person with the sweet tooth in the family, stop in at **Bateman's Jelly Shop** (704–586–9650) or pick up a gift for a hunter you know at **Duck Decoys, Inc.** (704–586–9000), which also carries sportswear and other unusual gifts.

CULLOWHEE

The **Mountain Heritage Center** is part of Western Carolina University in Cullowhee. To get here from Dillsboro, take Highway 107 south. The center promotes the rich tradition of the southern Appalachian Mountains through exhibits, educational programs, and demonstrations. Exhibits at the center present life in the mountains from yesterday and today. You'll see photographs, artifacts, relics, and other displays that relate to the migration of the Scotch-Irish people who settled the area in the eighteenth century. The center also presents temporary exhibits on mountain crafts and works such as blacksmithing as well as programs on the natural beauty of the area. Admission to the center is free. From April through October, the center is open from 8:00 A.M. to 5:00 P.M. Monday through Friday and 2:00 to 5:00 P.M. Sunday, except during university holidays. Call (704) 227–7129 for more information.

Thousands of people from across the Carolinas, Georgia, and Tennessee come to Cullowhee each September for **Mountain Heritage Day,** which is sponsored in part by the Mountain Heritage Center. Cullowhee comes alive with crafts, mountain music, food, storytelling, and more during this event. Admission and events are free. For more information, call the Mountain Heritage Center.

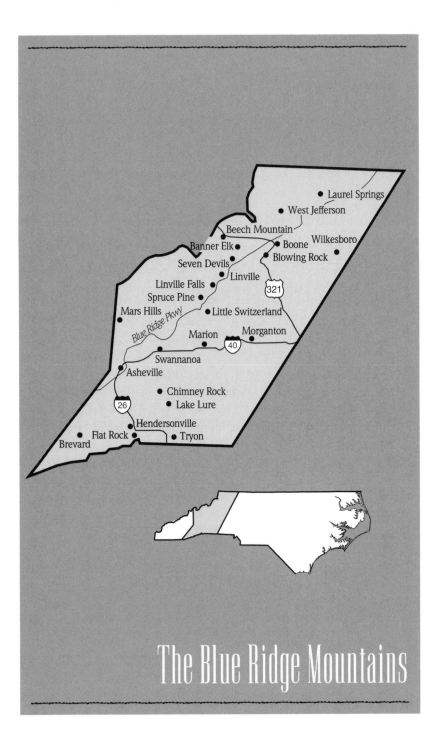

Laurel Springs

West Jefferson

Beech Mountain

Banner Elk ● ● Boone
Seven Devils Wilkesboro
Blowing Rock
Linville Falls ● Linville

Spruce Pine ● 321

Mars Hills
Little Switzerland

Blue Ridge Pkwy

Marion Morganton

40

Swannanoa

Asheville

26 Chimney Rock
Lake Lure

Hendersonville

Flat Rock Tryon
Brevard

The Blue Ridge Mountains

The Blue Ridge Mountains

You'll never know how much fun a waterfall can be until you go to North Carolina's Blue Ridge Mountains. In this land of waterfalls, each one is a beautiful sight, but one waterfall stands out from all the rest and promises hours of fun in the water for your family. In addition, Western North Carolina's biggest city, including one of the largest private residences in the United States, is here ready to provide great family adventure. This region also offers an opportunity to learn about some of the state's most prominent residents or to take a trip with the help of a llama.

Interstate 40 is the main route in the Blue Ridge from points east. Interstate 26 will get you here from the south. One of the main attractions here is the Blue Ridge Parkway, and you'll easily discover all the activities it has to offer in addition to the breathtaking views. If you're looking for quick travel, however, stick to the other highways because the parkway speed limit is 45 miles per hour.

BREVARD

Brevard and Transylvania County are known as the land of waterfalls. In fact, the word *Transylvania* means "across (*trans*) the woods (*sylvania*)," and it provides a perfect vacation opportunity if you're looking to get away from crowds and enjoy unspoiled beauty. The Davidson and French Broad rivers and their tributaries account for more than 250 waterfalls and 200 miles of cool mountain streams winding through the area. You can actually make a day out of visiting some of the lovely falls in this area. Start by heading west from Brevard on U.S. Highway 64, then south on State Highway 281 to **Whitewater Falls,** where you can hike the short trail for a panoramic view of the falls. At 441 feet, the upper falls of this two-level cascade are believed to be the highest in the eastern United States. Also on Highway 281, you'll find **Rainbow Falls,** which drop over 200 feet. On Highway 64 is **Toxaway Falls,** which cascades 123 feet, with the highway running across the top of them. For more information on some of the beautiful sites in this area, contact The Brevard/Transylvania County Visitor's Center at (800) 648–4523.

North of Brevard you head into **Pisgah National Forest,** which provides a wide range of camping facilities and great fishing streams. You'll find waterfalls here, too, and more adventure than you might expect. **Sliding Rock** was named just that for a reason. The 150-foot natural water slide is a favorite of visitors to the area who aren't afraid to get wet. It's an exhilarating blast as you speed down the huge rock along with the 11,000 gallons of 60-degree water that flow each minute. Your ride down the rock ends in a shallow pool, but if the kids want to make the slide, be sure they are strong swimmers. After your slide, stop by **Looking Glass Falls and Looking Glass Rock,** believed to be the largest single piece of granite in the southern Appalachians. You can park at the side of the road and walk down to the bottom of the 85-foot falls.

What would a national forest be if it didn't provide an opportunity to study nature? The **Cradle of Forestry** is a great hands-on museum that gets you on the road to discovering the wide variety of plant and animal life that inhabit this forest. Nearly 100 years ago the Cradle of Forestry was opened as the country's first school of forestry. The museum is now operated by the U.S. Forest Service and is a National Historic Site. It's located about 8 miles north of Brevard on the main forest road (Highway 276). In addition to the displays of plant and animal life, the museum also displays tools and other relics that relate to the history of the area. Young children will love learning about forest conservation at the Forest Fun Exhibit, where they can play with puzzles, puppets, and costumes. A touch-screen monitor lets them find more information on selected topics. Then head out on one of two nature trails that interpret more of the history of forestry and logging. On one trail you see an old logging locomotive. On another, occasional demonstrations of spinning, weaving, blacksmithing, and quilting are held. Admission to the museum costs $2.00 for adults and $1.00 for children ages six through seventeen. The museum is open from May through October from 10:00 A.M. to 6:00 P.M. daily. Call (704) 877–3130 for more information.

You can actually see why the trout fishing in this area is so good when you visit the **Pisgah Forest Fish Hatchery,** located in the forest, about 4 miles from Brevard. The hatchery breeds and raises brown and rainbow trout for stocking in area streams during the month of March, when no trout fishing is permitted. At the hatchery you can walk along the troughs the fish are raised in to see their various stages of growth. Displays in the center provide information on the hatchery and how the fish are raised. Admission is free. The hatchery is open to the public from 8:00 A.M. to 4:00 P.M. daily. Call (704) 877–3121 for more information.

HENDERSONVILLE

From Brevard, head east on Highway 64 to the juncture with U.S. Highway 25 to reach Hendersonville. Have you ever seen a talking tree? You will if you go to **Holmes Educational State Forest,** where they have a lot of them. Everyone in the family will get something out of your visit to the trails in the 235-acre forest. The short Talking Tree Trail features various hardwood trees that relate their origin and history on push-button tape recordings. Another trail, which is slightly longer at 3 miles, allows you to touch various forest objects in special boxes that give you a chance to guess what it is without seeing it. The forest is located about 8 miles south of Hendersonville and is open daily from April through November. Both picnic facilities and campsites are available in the forest, and park rangers present various interpretive programs throughout the year. Call (704) 692–0100 for more information.

A visit to **Historic Downtown Hendersonville** won't be a tremendously wild adventure, but you'll find a little something for everyone in the family. Main Street is beautifully adorned with seasonal plantings and benches scattered along the sidewalks, providing an opportunity for a short break or to sit back and people watch. Be sure to drop in at **Days Gone**

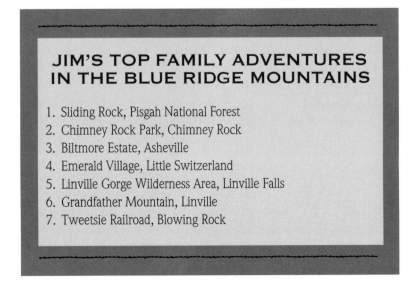

JIM'S TOP FAMILY ADVENTURES IN THE BLUE RIDGE MOUNTAINS

1. Sliding Rock, Pisgah National Forest
2. Chimney Rock Park, Chimney Rock
3. Biltmore Estate, Asheville
4. Emerald Village, Little Switzerland
5. Linville Gorge Wilderness Area, Linville Falls
6. Grandfather Mountain, Linville
7. Tweetsie Railroad, Blowing Rock

By, 303 North Main Street (704–693–9056), an old-fashioned drugstore that has been in town since 1882. After a drink or snack, head out to any one of the variety of stores downtown has to offer. You'll find everything from a specialty toy store to antiques to clothing stores and boutiques. Although some stores are open seven days a week, most shops are closed on Sunday. You can get more information on downtown Hendersonville and surrounding accommodations by calling the visitor center at (800) 828–4244.

North Carolina features a number of apple festivals, but downtown Hendersonville is the site of the "official" **North Carolina Apple Festival.** The festival is a four-day event that is usually held in early September. Downtown and the surrounding area come alive during the festival, which features sporting events, arts and crafts, entertainment, and of course lots of apples—applesauce, apple jelly, apple cider, and more. The celebration is highlighted by the King Apple Parade. Call (800) 828–4244 for more information.

If the hotels or inns in the area don't suit your needs, a good place to camp is **North Mills River and Campground,** located off State Highway

191 about 13 miles north of Hendersonville. In addition to fine fishing, the area offers picnic sites with grills and campsites for tents as well as trailers up to 22 feet. It's also a good place to take a trip down the river in an inner tube. Another plus this campground has to offer is the large, grassy playing area where the kids can run off some steam. The park, located in Pisgah National Forest and operated by the U.S. Forest Service, is open from early spring to late fall. A small fee is charged for overnight camping. Call (800) 283–2267 for more information.

FLAT ROCK

Flat Rock, south of Hendersonville on Highway 25, is one the oldest resort towns in the state and for more than twenty years was home to poet-historian Carl Sandburg. You can visit **Connemara: Carl Sandburg Home National Historic Site,** located west of Highway 25. Sandburg's works ranged widely, from children's books to stark political and social commentary, and his homesite offers insight into how he lived and worked. The home was built around 1838, and Sandburg moved into it in 1945 with his wife and daughters. While he wrote, his family managed to maintain the home as a working goat farm. The home has been largely preserved as it was when Sandburg died in 1967. More than 10,000 manuscripts, books, and notes are still scattered throughout the home. Admission is free, but guided tours cost $2.00 for anyone age seventeen or older. The site is open from 9:00 A.M. to 5:00 P.M. daily, but you'll want to call ahead for a schedule of guided tours. Call (704) 693–4178 for more information.

TRYON

From Flat Rock, head south on Highway 25 and east on Highway 176 to Tryon, located at the western edge of the Blue Ridge Mountains and the home of numerous equestrian events year-round. The **Foothills Equestrian Nature Center,** 500 Hunting Country Road, is host to most of these events and also includes nature trails and interpretive nature programs. Among the most popular events are the Tryon Horse Show, which has been held each June since 1929, and the Block House Steeplechase, which is held each April. Call the center at (704) 859–9021 for more information.

For a slow-paced trip, head to **Pearson's Falls,** located 4 miles north of Tryon off Highway 176. The falls, which cascade down a gentle 90-foot slope, are beautifully maintained by the Tryon Garden Club. The area includes several hundred acres of wildlife preserve and botanical gardens. Paths through 200 species of ferns and plants wind around the falls. Picnic facilities are available, but no fires are allowed. Admission costs $2.00 for adults and 50 cents for children ages six through twelve. Pearson's Falls is open from 10:00 A.M. to dusk daily.

The Green River, which runs from the center of Polk County, north of Tryon, to the county's eastern edge, provides a great opportunity to take an adventurous cruise in an inner tube or specially-made kayak. **Tube Express** (704–894–3929) and **Green River Cove Campground** (704–749–3781), both located off State Highway 9 (take State Highway 108 north out of Tryon to the junction with Highway 9 and continue north), can set you up with all the equipment you need for a trip down the river. While the pace of the Green River is slower than the white water of the rivers at higher elevations, there are several series of rapids that make it fun for the younger as well as older members of the family. The outfitters offer tube, raft, and inflatable "funyak" rentals as well as shuttle service so you can simply float back to your car. Trips range from 3 to 6 miles. Prices start at $3.00 per person, including tube rental and shuttle.

LAKE LURE

The 27-mile-long **Lake Lure** provides an opportunity for fishing, swimming, and boating. Located near Highway 74 (continue north up Highway 9 from the Green River), it's an upscale resort town. The lake is surrounded by an unusual mountain range that has been the cause of some interesting geological formations. Faults in the mountains have caused landslides and exposed caves in the rock along the upper slopes. In addition, **Bottomless Pools** have been created as a result of stream erosion in the underlying rock. Admission of $2.00 for adults and $1.00 for children ages seven through twelve is charged to see these privately owned pools. They are open from April through October, from 9:30 A.M. to 5:30 P.M. daily. Call (704) 625–4275 for more information.

CHIMNEY ROCK

On a clear day you can see almost 75 miles east as you stand on top of the 500-million-year-old rock at **Chimney Rock Park,** which is easy to find at its location on Highway 74 north of Lake Lure. Plan to spend at least several hours climbing on the rocks and exploring the caves at this great park. An elevator installed in the rock will take you up the equivalent of twenty-six stories to the top of Chimney Rock, or you can explore the outside of it on a unique hiking trail. As you walk along the trail, you can take a subterranean shortcut and hike on the walkways that take you from rock to rock. You can also climb down the wooden stairs to see a moonshiners' cave. Two other trails will take you to views of **Hickory Nut Falls,** which cascade down 404 feet. While you're at the park you'll enjoy panoramic, breathtaking views all around. Snacks are available at the top of Chimney Rock, and picnic facilities are also available. Admission costs $9.00 for adults and $4.50 for children ages six through fifteen. The ticket office is open from 8:30 A.M. to 4:30 P.M. daily, and the park remains open until 6:00 P.M. The park is open year-round except Thanksgiving, Christmas, and New Year's Day, but trails are closed from December through February.

ASHEVILLE

If you plan a trip to Asheville, western North Carolina's biggest city, plan on being here a while. With a population of about 67,000, it's a great place for family adventure—to escape the heat of summer, to enjoy the color of fall and spring, or to spend a cozy weekend during the winter holidays. Although Asheville, nestled at the edge of the Smoky Mountains where Interstates 26 and 40 cross, has become a cultural and educational center for the western part of the state, its mountainous beauty remains. For information on the area, contact the Asheville Travel and Tourism Office at (800) 257–5583.

A trip to North Carolina's mountains, or anywhere nearby, wouldn't be complete without seeing the **Biltmore Estate,** the 255-room French Renaissance mansion that is one of the largest private residences in the country. You'll be dazzled as you approach this 8,000-acre estate, located on Highway 25 just off Interstate 40, that was built by George Vanderbilt in 1895. Vanderbilt, the grandson of a railroad tycoon, originally bought more than 125,000 acres of land in this area, including what is now Pisgah National Forest. He is best known for having led an effort to manage forestry, instead of simply cutting down trees any time the logging companies needed them. The home includes more than 50,000 works of art, furnishings, and antiques, which Vanderbilt spent years collecting in Europe and the Orient. Among the works you'll see at the home are pieces by Renoir and Whistler, in addition to a chess table once owned by Napoleon Bonaparte.

The home was constructed over a five-year period and took a total of one million hours of labor, much of it from European designers whom Vanderbilt brought here. In addition to the twenty-two rooms in which the Vanderbilt family lived, the home also includes an indoor swimming pool and bowling alley. Your trip to the estate won't be complete without a visit to the winery, where sparkling, red, white, and rosé wines are produced. Finally, take a stroll around the lovely 40-acre gardens and pools. Admission

Biltmore Estate, built in 1895, may be the largest private residence in America. (Photo by J. Valentine, courtesy The Biltmore Co.)

to the estate varies according to season and according to seasonal attractions. Admission is $27.95 for adults, $21.00 for children ages ten through seventeen, and free for children younger than ten. The house is open from 9:00 A.M. to 6:00 P.M. daily, except Thanksgiving, Christmas, and New Year's Day. Call (800) 543–2961 for more information.

Adjacent to the Biltmore Estate is **Historic Biltmore Village,** a group of restored homes that now contain unique shops, restaurants, and galleries. At these shops you'll find everything from handcrafted jewelry and pottery to blown glass and fine art. Once Upon a Time features a huge selection of children's books as well toys, games, and children's music. Biltmore Village Dolls is a spectacular showcase for the doll collector in the family, and the Complete Naturalist features supplies for rock hounds, birdwatchers, and stargazers. In addition, the kids are certain to be drawn inside Biltmore Magic and Costume Shop, where they can see live demonstrations and get a start on doing magic themselves. In all, you'll find more than thirty shops and most likely something for everyone in the family. Biltmore Village Historic Museum presents photographs, maps, and artifacts on the history of the village. Most shops are open from 10:00 A.M. to 5:30 P.M. Monday through Saturday and 1:00 to 5:00 P.M. Sunday.

The next thing you'll want to do while in Asheville is pay a visit to **Pack Place,** the city's downtown center of arts, education, and science. It is located at 2 South Pack Square and includes several different attractions for visitors to the area. You can by a pass for all of Pack Place's attractions or buy tickets for only the ones you want to see. Admission to each of the four museums is $3.00 for adults, $2.50 for students ages sixteen and seventeen, $2.00 for children four through fifteen, and free for children younger than four. Your best bet is the day pass which costs $5.50 for adults and students, $3.50 for children four through fifteen, and is free for children younger than four. Call (704) 257–4500 for ticket price information.

The best family feature Pack Place has to offer is the **Health Adventure,** a spectacular interactive facility that leads you through dozens of exhibits and displays about the human body. Here you can touch a 5-foot-high brain and challenge your own gray matter in a display that introduces you to a number of creativity-testing games. Next, enter the Bodyworks gallery where you can try to jump to the heights of the likes of Michael

Jordan or take a journey through a giant replica of your bloodstream. At the Miracle of Life Gallery you'll learn all about heredity and life before birth. Children younger than eight will get a kick out of dressing up as cowboys, pirates, and other characters at the Creative PlaySpace. Here they can also put on a puppet show or take a slide down the giant tongue. The Health Adventure is open from 10:00 A.M. to 5:00 P.M. Tuesday through Saturday. During heavy travel time, the museum is also open from 1:00 to 5:00 P.M. Sunday. Call (704) 254–6373 for more information.

You'll find a shiny collection of minerals at the **Colburn Gem & Mineral Museum,** also located at Pack Place. You'll see a variety of North Carolina's native stones showcased here. Also on display are a 229-carat cut blue topaz and a 376-pound aquamarine crystal, plus a rock that actually bends. Museum hours are 10:00 A.M. to 5:00 P.M. Tuesday through Saturday and 1:00 to 5:00 P.M. Sunday, from June through October. Call (704) 254–7162 for more information.

If arts and culture are your thing, Pack Place features a fine art museum as well as a cultural center. Twentieth-century American art makes up the biggest permanent collection at the **Asheville Art Museum** (704–253–3227). That collection features a wide range of work from impressionists as well as contemporary abstract artists. The **YMI Cultural Center** (704–252–4614) is located in the former Young Men's Institute, which was founded by George Vanderbilt in 1893. Today it features a wide array of African-American artifacts, art, and other exhibits.

While you'll find Asheville offers the opportunity for a number of walking tours to various historic homes, two homes are located nearby that you won't want to miss. The **Thomas Wolfe Memorial,** located at Woodfin Street (the entrance is next to the Radisson Hotel), is the preserved childhood home of the world-famous author. The twenty-nine–room boardinghouse operated by Wolfe's mother is still furnished with some of the family's possessions and retains the Dixieland feel of the time he lived there. Although Wolfe left the home at age fifteen to attend school in Chapel Hill, he wrote about it in his novel *Look Homeward Angel,* published in 1929. Admission to the home costs $1.00 for adults and 50 cents for students; children age five or younger are admitted free. The site is open during the spring, summer, and fall 9:00 A.M. to 5:00 P.M. Monday through Saturday and 1:00 to 5:00 P.M. Sunday. During the winter it's open from 10:00 A.M. to 4:00 P.M. Tuesday through Saturday and 1:00 to 4:00 P.M. Sunday. Call (704) 253–8304 for more information.

Just a few miles north of Asheville, you can visit the **Zebulon B. Vance Birthplace.** The site is located on Reems Creek Road, just off Highway 25. Vance, born in 1830, was a revered U.S. senator and served as governor of North Carolina during the Civil War. His home takes you back to the pioneer farm life of the eighteenth century. The two-story pine log structure has been reconstructed around the original chimney. Some of the furnishings in the home belonged to the Vance family, and all of it is representative of the late eighteenth and early nineteenth centuries. You can also visit the museum, which includes exhibits relating Vance's life, and the six outbuildings that surround the house. Special living history re-creations are presented in the spring and in the summer. Admission is free. From April through October the site is open from 9:00 A.M. to 5:00 P.M. Monday through Saturday and 1:00 to 5:00 P.M. Sunday. Hours from November through March are 10:00 A.M. to 4:00 P.M. Tuesday through Saturday and 1:00 to 4:00 P.M. Sunday. Call (704) 645–6706 for more information.

See wildlife up close at the **Nature Center,** located just east of Asheville off Interstate 40. The center is a living nature museum that attempts to show how animals, the environment, and people work together to shape the world. At the center you can come face-to-face with a mountain lion and a gray or red wolf. You can see how to milk a cow, or you can pet a lamb. The center's "World Underground" exhibit shows you the importance of this unique environment, where you'll find more life than you might expect. Admission to the center costs $4.00 for adults and $2.00 for kids ages three through thirteen. During the summer the center is open from 10:00 A.M. to 5:00 P.M. daily. During the winter the hours are the same except it's closed on Mondays. Call (704) 298–5600 for more information.

More natural beauty awaits at the **Botanical Gardens at Asheville,** on Weaver Boulevard near the University of North Carolina at Asheville. Here you'll find hundreds of species of plants and flowers that are native to the southern Appalachian mountains. Within these 10 acres you'll find a large azalea garden and a charming rock garden. In addition, you can see the renovated earthworks for the Battle of Asheville as well as a garden for the blind. Admission is free. The facility is open daily during daylight hours. Call (704) 252–5190 for more information.

While you'll have your choice of a variety of accommodations in and around Asheville, clearly the best place to stay is the **Grove Park Inn Resort** at 290 Macon Avenue. The resort is a grand hotel, first opened in 1913 and nestled in the hills of the Blue Ridge. In this hotel, made of huge local granite stones, there are 510 guest rooms, including twelve suites in the main building and the two wings. You can also play a round of golf on the eighteen-hole course, play tennis inside or out, swim inside or out, or rent a mountain bike from the fitness center. Planned children's programs are also scheduled from week to week. Rates start at around $150 per night in season. Call (800) 438–5800 for more information.

In Asheville you'll find the most-used entrance to the Blue Ridge Parkway, which runs from the Great Smoky Mountains National Park near Cherokee into Virginia at Interstate 77. You'll find a great deal to do along the parkway, and the section near Asheville is no exception. In addition to some beautiful overlooks, the biggest parkway attraction in this area is the **Folk Art Center,** at Parkway Milepost 382. Opened in 1980, this is southern Appalachia's oldest and best-known craft shop. The center is operated by the Southern Highland Craft Guild, the Appalachian Regional Commission, and the National Park Service. The 30,000-square-foot center is also one of the largest crafts shops you will find. A museum in the upstairs portion of the center is dedicated to displaying changing exhibits created by its members. You'll also have an opportunity to purchase quilts, toys, furniture, and stoneware made by member artisans. In addition, live demonstrations are held most of the time the center is open. Admission is free. From January through March, the center is open from 9:00 A.M. to 5:00 P.M. daily. From April through December, the center is open from 9:00 A.M. to 6:00 P.M. daily; closed Thanksgiving, Christmas, and New Year's Day. Call (704) 298–7928 for more information.

Drive about another twenty minutes eastward on the Blue Ridge Parkway and you come to **Craggy Gardens,** located between mileposts 363 and 369. The gardens are a beautifully sculptured sight when colorful rhododendron are at their peak bloom in early summer. Here you'll see a wide variety of other mountain wildflowers as well. You'll also find a visitor center, nature trails, and picnic facilities. Admission is free. Craggy Gardens is open daily from May through October, generally during daylight hours. Call (704) 298–0398 for more information.

From the gardens you are only a few minutes away from **Mount Mitchell State Park,** which, at 6,684 feet, is the tallest peak east of the Mississippi River. It pokes out of the Black Mountains, which are among the oldest on earth. From an observation tower at Mount Mitchell's peak, you can see the Smoky Mountains. You'll also find a small museum as well as a restaurant that's open in the summer. In addition, you can enjoy a number of outdoor activities at the 1,600-acre park, including hiking, picnicking, and some camping. The park is open according to weather conditions, so call ahead (704–675–4611) if you want to visit in the fall or winter. Admission is free. To get there, exit off Blue Ridge Parkway at mile post 355 onto State Highway 128.

SWANNANOA

A great way to really get back to nature and to take in the beauty of the Blue Ridge is by way of llama. That's right! You and your family can rent a llama, a pack animal that became domesticated in South America, for a day or overnight trip. **Avalon Llama Treks,** 450 Old Buckeye Cove Road in Swannanoa, east of Asheville off U.S. Highway 70, provides a variety of expeditions from brunch and dinner trips to fishing and camping trips. They provide all camping gear and will send you a list of what you need to bring when you make reservations. Since a llama can carry up to 90 pounds, there is almost no limit to what you can bring on your trip. Single-meal trips start at $45 per person, day trips cost $65 per person, and overnight trips cost $100 per person. Call (704) 299–7155 for more information or to make reservations.

MARS HILL

Before you leave the Asheville area you can get in a little skiing only about forty minutes away at **Ski Wolf Laurel.** Located north of Asheville on Highway 23, Wolf Laurel features fifteen slopes with a wide variety of difficulty for various skill levels. In addition, the ski school there features SKIWEE, a special program for children ages four through seven. Not only will your children get simple lessons and instructions, they will get practice through races, games, and other planned activities. The lodge here is nice, too. The resort has food ranging from snacks to full meals, in a restaurant that provides beautiful views of the slopes. Accommodations are available at **Wolf Laurel Inn** as well as at vacation homes that surround the area. Snow-making machines allow this slope to open late in November. Adult lift ticket rates start at $15.00 for a half day and $30.00 for a full day. Children age eight or younger are half price, and children nine through twelve get $3.00 off the adult rates. Equipment rental starts at $8.00 for a half day and $12.00 for a full day. The SKIWEE school costs $35.00 for a half day and $50.00 for a full day. Call (800) 817–4111 for more information.

SPRUCE PINE

If you're looking for a scenic drive, make your way back from Mars Hill to the Blue Ridge Parkway by taking Highway 19 north, then east to Highway 80 south, or you can head straight over to Spruce Pine by staying on Highway 19. As you cruise through these mountain highways, you'll see that they are lined with handicraft shops and galleries, where you usually see local crafters and artists at work. If you want to see more, you can obtain a guidebook for a scenic drive that highlights this local work by contacting the Yancey County Chamber of Commerce at (704) 682–7413. In addition to the local crafts, this area's biggest attraction is its mines. **Gem Mountain,** located on State Highway 226 in Spruce Pine, features flumes where you can hunt for gems for a small fee. In addition, you can visit Gem Mountain's Sands of Time museum, have a picnic by the stream, eat at the restaurant, or enjoy an ice-cream cone. Gem Mountain is open from March through December from 9:00 A.M. to 5:00 P.M. daily (until 7:00 P.M. during the summer). Call (704) 765–6130 for more information.

LITTLE SWITZERLAND

Everything that makes the mountains of North Carolina so great—the crafts, the mines, the beautiful scenery, the lodging, the shopping, and the dining—can be found in Little Switzerland, not far south of Spruce Pine down Highway 226. **Emerald Village,** located on McKinney Mine Road off Highway 226A, is probably one of the biggest and most popular public mining operations in the mountains. Dozens of different minerals, gems, and rocks have been found here, including aquamarine, emerald, garnet, and uranium. Attendants are on hand to help you identify your finds, as are artisans for cutting and mounting your stones. Additionally, you can visit the **North Carolina Mining Museum,** located in an underground mine, where you'll see old mining equipment and displays on the area's mining heritage. Cost of mining varies. The museum admission is $3.50 for adults and $2.50 for children and students age seventeen or younger. Other free village attractions include the Company Store and Discovery Mill, where you'll see more displays related to mining as well as souvenirs and gifts. Emerald Village is open from 9:00 A.M. to 6:00 P.M. daily and from 9:00 A.M. to 5:00 P.M. daily from Memorial Day to Labor Day the rest of the year.

MARION

South of Little Switzerland off Highway 126 is a popular lake noted for its outdoor activities. **Lake James State Park** is a great place to play golf, fish, camp, swim, and hike. The lake, which is fed by two mountain streams and the Catawba River, offers 150 miles of shoreline along beautiful crystal-clear water. Ten golf courses are located in this area, and the park contains great campsites for low-impact camping. Each site has a grill, water, and a picnic table, and the sites are located away from traffic. Along the park's nature trails you never know when you'll get a glimpse of a deer, flying squirrel, fox, or muskrat, and the lake offers great bass, crappie, and catfish fishing. The park is open year-round, and admission is free. You can call the park at (704) 652–5047 for more information.

LINVILLE FALLS

Located just off the Blue Ridge Parkway on U.S. Highway 221 is the town of Linville Falls and the **Linville Gorge Wilderness Area.** These 7,600 acres of land have been preserved as a natural area, but you can hike a number of trails for various views of the falls and the Linville River, which descends more than 2,000 feet in only 12 miles. The upper falls roll over 50 feet and disappear into the mountain, then the lower falls drop another 60 feet. If it's hot, you can hike down the rocks bordering the falls and wade in the cool waters, watching more adventurous hikers scale the vertical rocks. The gorge below the falls is part of Pisgah National Forest and is maintained for hunting and fishing. Two observation points, one on the east and one on the west, provide excellent panoramic views of the gorge. You'll also come across plenty of picnic facilities around this area.

It's impossible to ignore the signs urging you to visit **Linville Caverns,** where the 52-degree year-round temperature is more than welcome during a humid North Carolina summer. The caverns, the only ones in the state that are open to the public, are located on Highway 221 near its intersection with the Blue Ridge Parkway. At the caverns you'll get a lesson on stalagmites, stalactites, and other natural formations. In addition, you'll see unusual blind fish in the underground stream and experience total darkness. Guided tours on the marked trail are held about every half hour. Admission is $4.00 for adults and $2.50 for children ages five through twelve. From March through October the caverns are open from 9:00 A.M. to 5:00 P.M. daily (until 6:00 P.M. in the summer). Hours during the rest of the year are 9:00 A.M. to 4:30 P.M. Saturday and Sunday. Call (704) 756–4171 for more information.

LINVILLE

Don't let the similarity in names confuse you—Linville and Linville Falls are two different towns. Linville, north of Linville Falls on Highway 221, is known for what is probably the top scenic attraction in the North Carolina Mountains—**Grandfather Mountain.** This is a great place to spend the day hiking and learning about nature. The 5,964-foot peak was named for its profile as it appears from about 7 miles north. As the name suggests, from this vantage point the mountain looks like a bearded grandfather. Grandfather Mountain has been recognized by the United Nations as an international reserve where people and nature live together in harmony. You enter the park off Highway 221 and can drive through a lot of it, but you'll have to park at the visitor center and walk to get to the top. You'll also find picnic and camping facilities here.

A good time to visit Grandfather Mountain is the second weekend in July, when the **Highland Games** are held. While there are other Scottish celebrations in the state, this is one of the best. It includes traditional

Scottish athletic competitions, spiced up with authentic Scottish music, dance, and other attractions from the Scottish tradition. For more information on the Highland Games, call (704) 733–1333.

But no matter what time of year you visit Grandfather Mountain, there is always plenty to do. As you drive into the park, the first attraction you come to is the nature museum, a small museum with a gift shop that kids will adore. At the shop they will find toys and all sorts of knickknacks related to animals, nature, and the Blue Ridge Parkway. The museum offers an unusual look at the area's natural past with displays and films on nature and the mountains. You see gold nuggets, precious gemstones, a billion-year-old rock, and displays of rare plants and animals. The kids will surely want to have their picture taken with the big bear. They'll also love the Daniel Boone exhibit. Probably the most popular attraction at Grandfather Mountain is the **Mile-High Swinging Bridge.** It extends majestically over a natural gorge filled with hardwood trees and rhododendron. You'll find overlooks on both sides of the bridge if you can't make the walk across. Finally, your family will get a chance to feed the bears that inhabit a huge natural den. A variety of animals—including black bears and cubs, cougars, deer, and eagles—are on display in their natural habitats. Many have been injured and will never be able to return to the wild.

Admission to the Grandfather Mountain complex costs $9.00 for adults and $5.00 for children ages four to twelve. In the winter, the facility is open from 8:00 A.M. to 5:00 P.M. daily; spring and fall hours are 8:00 A.M. to 6:00 P.M. daily; summer hours are 8:00 A.M. to 7:00 P.M. daily; closed Thanksgiving and Christmas. Ticket sales stop one hour before closing, but you'll want to spend several hours at Grandfather Mountain. Call (800) 468–7325 for more information.

SEVEN DEVILS

Just north of Linville on State Highway 105 is **Hawksnest Golf and Ski Resort** in Seven Devils. This year-round resort not only has become known for one of the steepest slopes among the North Carolina ski areas but is also popular among a new breed of snowboarders. Ten slopes are available as well as lessons and rentals. Traditionally, the resort has offered the better deals early in the season. From opening day, in late November to early December, until the end of December, Hawksnest has specials as low as $20 for lift tickets, rentals, and lessons. Visitors can enjoy the golf course during the more temperate months. Call (800) 822–4295 for more information.

BANNER ELK

To the north of Linville is a skier's paradise. Between 5 and 8 feet of natural snow fall in this area each winter, depending on the elevation, but snow-making machines provide good skiing conditions all winter long. You can call the High Country Ski Report at (800) 962–2322 to get conditions at all three of the area's ski resorts. Traveling north on Highway 105, the first ski area you come to is **Sugar Mountain,** in Banner Elk. This resort is the largest, with eighteen slopes and eight lifts. A 1,200-foot drop provides plenty of thrills for the advanced skier, while lessons are offered for beginners. Lift ticket rates start at $25 for a full day and $17 for nights. Rentals start at $10. Call (704) 898–5256 for more information.

BEECH MOUNTAIN

Ski Beech, located on Highway 184 in Beech Mountain, north of Banner Elk, is at the highest elevation of the area's ski resorts and as a result offers the most natural snow. But in addition, snow-making machines provide prime skiing all winter long. Here fourteen slopes and eleven lifts tend to keep you on the slope more. Skaters in the family will appreciate the ice-skating rink here and special programs are offered for children. Prices start at $25 for a full day and $15 at night. Rentals start at $10. Call (800) 438–2093 for more information.

BOONE

Boone is a great central location for seeing this part of the Blue Ridge. Not only is there a lot to see and do in and around the city, but it also provides easy access to the Blue Ridge Parkway, the ski resorts, and other towns and attractions. From Banner Elk, take State Highway 194 east. From Linville, take the Blue Ridge Parkway to U.S. Highway 321. Boone is named for the famous frontiersman Daniel Boone, who had a cabin here from 1760 to 1769. Today there are thousands of lodging rooms ranging from bed-and-breakfast inns to chain hotels. The Boone Convention and Visitor's Bureau (800–852–9506) can assist you with finding accommodations.

Boone's legacy and contribution to the settlement of the area is portrayed in **Horn in the West,** a fabulous musical outdoor drama, held at the amphitheater just off U.S. Highway 421. The play, America's third longest running outdoor drama, is set during the time Boone lived here, when colonial unrest against British dominance was at its peak. The play reveals how Boone and his men struggled to settle this area and built the mountain culture that is still evident today. A favorite from the piece, for young and old alike, is a spectacular Cherokee Indian fire dance. Performances, which last about two hours, are held at 8:30 P.M. Tuesday through Sunday from late June to mid-August. Tickets cost $9.00 for adults and $4.50 for children age thirteen or younger. Call (704) 264–2120 for more information.

You can head to the outdoor theater early to see the **Daniel Boone Native Gardens,** which features plantings unique to the area, native gardens, and unique architecture, and the **Hickory Ridge Homestead Museum,** a log village representative of the type of eighteenth-century community the frontier settlers created. Costumed guides will lead you through the museum where you see demonstrations of how these settlers lived. The gardens and museum are open from 1:00 to 8:30 P.M. while the show is in production. The cost is $2.00 for adults and $1.00 for children age thirteen or younger.

The **Appalachian Cultural Heritage Museum,** located on University Hall Drive just off Highway 321, is a great little museum that features exhibits and audiovisual displays of not only the past but the present as well. Here you see antique quilts, arrowheads, handmade furniture, Junior Johnson's race car, and a bit of the yellow brick road from the *Land of Oz,* a former theme park based on the movie. Admission is $2.00 for adults and $1.00 for students ages twelve through eighteen. The museum is open from 10:00 A.M. to 5:00 P.M. Tuesday through Saturday and 1:00 to 5:00 P.M. Sunday.

If it's time for dinner, make sure you're hungry before you head to the **Daniel Boone Inn Restaurant,** located at the juncture of highways 321 and 421. One price gets you all you want to eat at this charming, rustic inn. Children four through six eat for $1.95, seven through eleven for

$3.95, and twelve and older for $10.95. Children younger than four eat free. You won't have to worry about menus or deciding what you're going to eat because meals are served family-style just like at Grandma's house. If they run out of mashed potatoes, don't worry—when you get seconds you can have rice. There is plenty of variety on the dessert cart, so save room if you can. Call (704) 264–8657 for more information.

To schedule an active family adventure without doing all the planning yourself, call **Wahoo's Adventures,** located on Highway 321. No matter what kind of adventure you are looking for, they can help you put it all together. White-water rafting trips are offered on four rivers in the area for all different ages and skill levels. Full- and half-day trips are conducted, and gourmet picnics are prepared for you by the crew. If an overnight trip is more to your liking, that can be arranged. The outfitter also plans four-wheel-drive trips, self-guided canoe trips, inner-tubing, and ski trips. Prices are as varied as the activities, so call ahead for information or to make reservations at (800) 444–7238.

BLOWING ROCK

Blowing Rock, south of Boone on Highway 321, is a small resort town, and you'll find plenty near here. Plan to spend several hours in the village shopping center downtown. There are a dozen antique shops, a great sports novelty shop, and local craftworkers making candles and other items. Just south of the shopping district on Highway 321 you can learn how the town got its name at the **Blowing Rock,** where it snows upside down. The attraction is a large rock formation hanging over John's River Gorge. Plan to spend about an hour or so enjoying the views and walking the ridges and rock, as you discover the story of this mysterious formation. Legend says that a Cherokee brave who had thrown himself off the Blowing Rock was blown up out of the gorge to the Chickasaw maiden who had prayed for his return for three days. Today, light objects thrown from the rock will be blown back up. Admission costs $3.00 for adults and $1.00 for children ages six through eleven; children younger than six are admitted free. In March and April, the attraction is open from 9:00 A.M. to 5:00 P.M. daily. From May through October, it's open from 8:00 A.M. to 8:00 P.M. daily. Call (704) 295–7111 for more information.

You might think they need to beef up security when you take a ride on the **Tweetsie Railroad,** because it seems robberies occur on every single trip. Tweetsie, located just north of Blowing Rock, is a great theme park where you take a trip back to the Old West. You'll enjoy dozens of great rides as you walk through the theme park, where you are more than likely to meet up with a gunslinger or an Indian chief. You can also visit a turn-of-the-century general store, a blacksmith shop, and a jail. Another option is a mining town, where the children can pan for gold or meet the animals in the petting zoo. But the biggest attraction here is old Number 12, a steam locomotive that takes you on a 3-mile journey around a mountain. You never know when those robbers or even Indians will hop on board, so stay alert. Plenty of traditional theme park rides provide hours of entertainment as well. In October you can enjoy a haunted house, visit a mad scientist's lab, and go trick-or-treating at the **Tweetsie Railroad Halloween Festival,** which features rides on the ghost train. Admission to Tweetsie costs $13 for adults and $11 for children ages four through twelve. The theme park is open from Memorial Day through October from 9:00 A.M. to 6:00 P.M. daily. Call (800) 526–5740 for more information.

As you drove to Tweetsie from Blowing Rock on Highway 321, you probably noticed **Mystery Hill,** a hands-on science museum that lets you decide if these strange exhibits are natural phenomena or illusions. It's worth stopping here to see rocks that glow in the dark and exhibits that defy gravity or leave your shadow on the wall. Admission costs $5.00 for adults and $4.00 for children ages five through twelve. Mystery Hill is open from 8:00 A.M. to 8:00 P.M. daily from Memorial Day through Labor Day and from 9:00 A.M. to 5:00 P.M. daily the rest of the year. Call (704) 264–2792 for more information.

The Blowing Rock area is one of the best places to explore the Blue Ridge Parkway. Nearby you'll find a small lake where you can rent canoes and paddleboats, plus two great parks where you can have a picnic and let the kids run. **Moses Cone Memorial Park,** located at milepost 297, has grills at the sites, stepping-stones in the stream that runs through the park, and a big field that's great for tossing a football or baseball. **Julian Price Park,** also located at milepost 297, features great hiking trails around the lake as well as boat rentals. Just south of the park is the **Linn Cove**

Viaduct, the most complicated concrete bridge in the world. It took 15 million pounds of concrete and steel to wind the road around the cove without damaging the environment.

Just off the parkway near Highway 321 you'll find another of North Carolina's ski resorts. **Appalachian Ski Mountain** has nine slopes and four lifts and was rated by the *Charlotte Observer* as the best slope for learning how to ski. The resort is home of the French-Swiss Ski College. The resort traditionally offers the best rate during its opening anniversary period, when you ski for 1962 rates of $5.00 for an adult lift ticket, $2.50 for a junior lift ticket, and rentals for $6.50. Look for this special deal early in December. The rest of the season, the rates are in line with other resorts. Call (800) 322–2373 for more information.

WEST JEFFERSON

Headed north on the Blue Ridge Parkway you escape a lot of the common tourist activity that you find in the larger towns. **Mount Jefferson State Park** on Highway 221 offers facilities for picnics, hiking, and a chance to study nature at this small, 539-acre facility. But the most popular attraction here is the collection of contemporary paintings by Ben Long at two local churches. **The Blue Ridge Mountain Frescoes,** at St. Mary's Episcopal Church in West Jefferson and Holy Trinity Episcopal Church in nearby Glendale Springs, include *The Last Supper,* one of the largest frescoes in the country, and *Mary Great with Child.* Admission is free, and the churches are open to the public during limited hours. Call (910) 982–3076 for more information.

Another interesting place to visit in West Jefferson is the **Ashe County Cheese Factory,** located on Main Street in West Jefferson. Founded in 1930, it is North Carolina's only cheese factory. Forty-five– minute tours of the plant are conducted by the staff there, who will show you how they make cheese. They demonstrate how they turn milk into Cheddar, Colby, and several other types of cheese. Admission is free. The factory is open to the public from 8:30 A.M. to 5:00 P.M. Monday through Friday, but you should get there by 2:00 P.M. to see them making cheese. One day a week they usually don't have milk, so call ahead at (910) 246–2501 for more information.

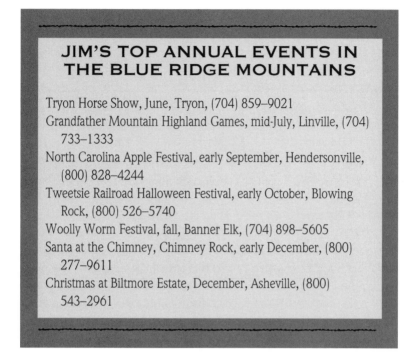

JIM'S TOP ANNUAL EVENTS IN THE BLUE RIDGE MOUNTAINS

Tryon Horse Show, June, Tryon, (704) 859–9021

Grandfather Mountain Highland Games, mid-July, Linville, (704) 733–1333

North Carolina Apple Festival, early September, Hendersonville, (800) 828–4244

Tweetsie Railroad Halloween Festival, early October, Blowing Rock, (800) 526–5740

Woolly Worm Festival, fall, Banner Elk, (704) 898–5605

Santa at the Chimney, Chimney Rock, early December, (800) 277–9611

Christmas at Biltmore Estate, December, Asheville, (800) 543–2961

LAUREL SPRINGS

At Blue Ridge Parkway milepost 241 near Laurel Springs, you'll find the largest recreation area on the Parkway, **Doughton Park.** The park includes all the standard park facilities, and you can also stay at **Bluffs Lodge,** a rustic lodge that offers twenty-four rooms with scenic views of the mountains and surrounding meadows. A coffee shop and craft shop are located nearby. Here you can explore great scenic trails and several historic buildings. The park is open from May through October. Rates at the lodge start at around $60 per night. Call (910) 372–4499 for more information.

WILKESBORO

Worth a detour south off the Blue Ridge Parkway from Laurel Springs is the Wilkesboro area. The **W. Kerr Scott Dam and Reservoir,** located on the Yadkin River, is accessible by taking State Highway 18 through Wilkesboro to State Highway 268 west. This 1,470-acre lake at the edge of the Blue Ridge Mountains offers a dozen sites for outdoor recreation. There are more than 55 miles of shoreline for everything from swimming to boating. Picnic facilities are located throughout the area, and you can also camp at many of these sites. **Berry Mountain Park,** located 5 miles west of Wilkesboro on Highway 268, is a good place to spend the day swimming and sunning on the beach. **Bloodcreek Overlook,** located about 2 more miles west, has a fishing pier as well as picnic facilities that include grills. A state fishing license is required to fish here. Call (910) 921–3750 for more information.

You can make an appointment or take yourself on a walking tour of **Old Wilkes,** which includes thirteen buildings that are in the National Register of Historic Places. Some of the highlights on the tour are the Old Wilkes Jail, completed in 1860, which once held Tom Dooley, convicted of murdering his girlfriend and made famous in his ballad; Wilkes County Courthouse, a 1902 classical revival building that is known for the Tory Oak on the front lawn, from which British sympathizers were hung; and the Robert Cleveland House, a log home built in the 1770s and moved behind the jail. Call (910) 667–3712 for more information.

MORGANTON

You can end your tour by swinging back west and south from Wilkesboro along Highway 18 to the juncture with Interstate 40 at Morganton, the home of the late U.S. Senator Sam Ervin, Jr., who became famous for presiding over the Watergate hearings. This area offers a number of opportunities for recreational outdoor activities. **Tuttle Educational State Forest,** located north of Morganton off Highway 64, is a 170-acre park that offers a range of educational nature programs. In addition, there is a family campground as well as primitive campsites. South of Morganton off Highway 18 is **South Mountains State Park,** a great place for trout fishing or simply wading in the streams or stepping on stones. The 7,330 acres in this park are largely undeveloped, but a series of bridges and walkways along the trails make the park more accessible, especially for younger children. Both sites are open during daylight hours generally year-round. Contact Tuttle Educational Forest at (704) 433–4772 and South Mountains at (704) 757–5608 for more information.

The Northern Piedmont

Some of North Carolina's biggest metropolitan areas are located in the Northern Piedmont, and as a result there is no shortage of great things to see and do. Educational opportunities abound at the state capital and on the campuses of the state's leading universities. Here you'll also find one of the country's leading zoos, where you can come within an arm's length of a rare bird or any number of African and North American animals. In addition, some of the best parks are located here, as is a living-history eighteenth-century Moravian village.

The highway system here is tops. You won't have much problem navigating this area. Interstate 40 takes you here from the west and combines with Interstate 85 at Greensboro. Interstate 40 then runs south through Raleigh and Interstate 85 runs north into Virginia.

HICKORY

Leaving the Blue Ridge Mountains, you descend quickly into the Catawba River Valley, originally inhabited by the Catawba Indians, the "people of the river." The Hickory area, the westernmost point of the Northern Piedmont, is the first city you come to and has become known as one of the state's national furniture capitals. So if you are looking for new or antique furniture, this is the place to come. In addition to the many stores you'll find throughout the area, the **Hickory Furniture Mart,** located at 2220 Highway 70 East, features sixty-five factory stores, outlets, and galleries. In

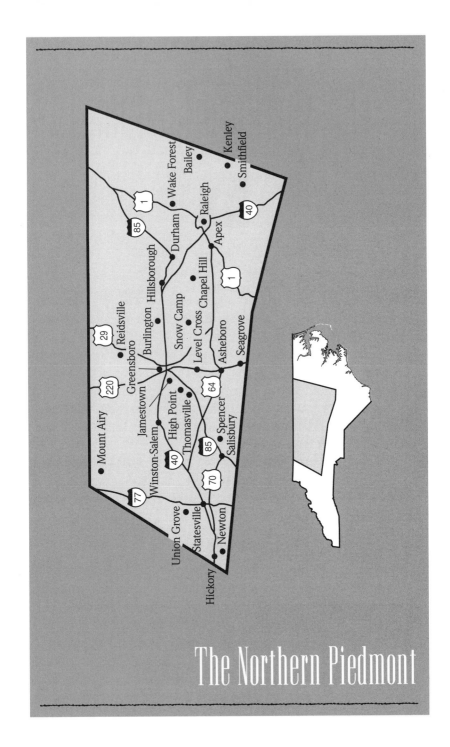

The Northern Piedmont

the 12 acres of showrooms you find everything you need to decorate your home, including bedding, linens, art, floor coverings, and furniture. Adjacent to the mart is an antiques center that includes North Carolina furniture as well as Oriental and European pieces. If shopping for furniture doesn't hold the kid's attention for very long, they might like learning more about the furniture industry that has been so important for this area for so long. The **Catawba Valley Furniture Museum** is located at the Furniture Mart. The museum traces the roots of the industry and features a reproduction of an early woodworking shop as well as a collection of vintage tools and furniture. Both attractions are open from 9:00 A.M. to 6:00 P.M. Monday through Friday and 9:00 A.M. to 5:00 P.M. Saturday. Admission is free. Call (800) 462–6278 for more information.

Hickory also offers a fine center to learn about arts and science. The **Catawba Science Center** and the **Hickory Museum of Art,** both located at 243 Third Ave, will provide hours of entertainment and education. The science center features a wide variety of hands-on exhibits. Don't miss the Hall of Life Science's exhibit on the life cycle of a live mountain stream or the Bodyworks' exhibits on health and fitness. The Physical Science Arcade offers opportunities to learn about physics, light, and sound. The art museum's permanent and traveling exhibits include nineteenth-century as well as contemporary art. Admission to both attractions is free. The centers are open from 10:00 A.M. to 5:00 P.M. Tuesday through Friday, 10:00 A.M. to 4:00 P.M. Saturday, and 1:00 to 4:00 P.M. Sunday. Call the science center at (704) 322–8169 and the art museum at (704) 327–8576 for more information.

NEWTON

East and a bit south of Hickory is the town of Newton, the county seat, located off Interstate 40. Here you'll find a number of historically significant sites on the **Historic Newton Walking Tour,** which includes 105 buildings. Among the sites on the tour are **Murray's Mill,** a fully restored corn and gristmill and **St. Paul's Lutheran Church,** a two-story log, weatherboarded church that includes the balcony where slaves sat during services and a cemetery with tombstones in German dating back to 1771. Also on the tour is the **Catawba County Museum of History,** located in the

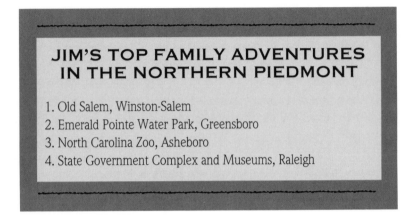

JIM'S TOP FAMILY ADVENTURES IN THE NORTHERN PIEDMONT

1. Old Salem, Winston-Salem
2. Emerald Pointe Water Park, Greensboro
3. North Carolina Zoo, Asheboro
4. State Government Complex and Museums, Raleigh

Catawba County Courthouse downtown. Interesting exhibits there include a jail cell, artifacts tracing the history of the valley, a 1930 race car, a 1770 British officer's red coat, and Civil War memorabilia. Admission is free but donations are accepted at the museum, which is open from 9:00 A.M. to 4:00 P.M. Tuesday through Friday and 2:00 to 5:00 P.M. Sunday. Call (704) 465–0383 for more information. For a walking tour brochure call (704) 465–7400.

STATESVILLE

Continue east on Interstate 40 or Highway 70 to where they intersect Interstate 77 and you'll be in Statesville. State Highways 64 and 21 also converge here. Balloons fill the sky over Statesville each September as one of the oldest and biggest balloon rallies on the East Coast gets underway. The **National Balloon Rally,** held the third weekend of September, is the city's best attraction. Thousands of spectators show up annually to watch the beautiful, silent, colorful balloons ascend to the heavens. More than 100 teams show up for the event. Standard festival amenities are also offered at the rally. Call the Statesville Travel and Tourism Board at (704) 521–3666 for more information about the balloon rally or other special events.

Whether you are in Statesville for the balloon rally or just passing through, take a couple hours to visit the new **Children's Museum of**

Iredell County. Located originally at 501 South Mulberry Street, the museum moved to 134 Court Street in 1996 and is dedicated primarily to providing education in visual arts, drama, literature, and music to local children. When completed, the museum will present performances, by both professionals and local students, throughout the year. In addition, exhibits that include Handy Sandy's Hardware and Repair, the Great Pretender Costume Shops, and the Rainbow Art Room are planned. Admission to the museum is free, but the shows will cost $5.00 per person. The museum is open during the school year from 1:00 to 5:00 P.M. Wednesday and Thursday and from 10:00 A.M. to 2:00 P.M. Saturday. During the summer, it's open from 10:00 A.M. to 2:00 P.M. Wednesday and Thursday and 10:00 A.M. to 2:00 P.M. Saturday. Call (704) 872–4773 for more information.

Another museum, the **Arts and Science Center,** located in an old pumping station built in 1899 on Museum Road, is dedicated to promoting arts, history, and nature. The most interesting exhibit is a 2,000-year-old Egyptian mummy. Many of the other exhibits rotate and include displays on natural science, art, Native Americans, toys, and various collections. There are several nature trails surrounding the museum, with one featuring a pioneer settlement. Admission is free, but donations are accepted. The center is open from 10:00 A.M. to 5:00 P.M. Tuesday through Saturday and 2:00 to 5:00 P.M. Sunday. It's closed on major holidays and during the week around Christmas. Call (704) 873–4734 for more information.

In addition to science and the arts, history is alive in Statesville. Just north on Highway 21 is **Fort Dobbs,** built in 1756 in honor of Royal Colonial Governor Arthur Dobbs. The fort was constructed at a time when tension between the colonists and the British was reaching its height and settlers came into increasing conflict with Indians. On many occasions colonists in the area were forced out of their homes and sought refuge at the fort, which was attacked only once in more than fifteen years. Today the fort, which includes little more than ruins and ground impressions, is the site of continual archeological investigation. Archeological finds and other artifacts are displayed along the trails and at the visitor center. Admission is free. From April through October the site is open from 9:00 A.M. to 5:00 P.M. Monday through Saturday and 1:00 to 5:00 P.M. Sunday. From

November through March the site is open from 10:00 A.M. to 4:00 P.M. Tuesday through Saturday and 1:00 to 4:00 P.M. Sunday. Call (704) 873–5866 for more information.

During the summer months Statesville's **Love Valley Arena,** located off Highway 115, features old-fashioned rodeos and other events. Love Valley is known throughout the state as a cowboy's paradise, and it attracts horse enthusiasts all year round. During the **Tar Heel Classic Horse Show,** held in May, you can get a look at Tennessee Walkers, Arabians, and quarter horses as they go through various events and judging. Among the fun-filled rodeo events are junior competitions and events with a frontier theme. Call (704) 592–7451 for more information.

UNION GROVE

One of the state's more unusual annual events is the **Old Time Fiddler's and Bluegrass Convention** held each May near the town of Union Grove, located north of Statesville off Interstate 77 on State Highway 901. It is the oldest event of its kind in the nation and attracts musicians from around the country. The weekendlong event features continuous performances and competitions in all areas of bluegrass music, from clogging to fiddling. Whether you're an experienced fiddler wishing to sharpen your skills or a beginner who's never held a fiddle before, the convention has a class—and often an instrument—available for you. Booths are situated throughout the campground, offering a variety of musical and craft items for sale. Admission to the convention and to the classes is free. For more information, contact the Statesville Travel and Tourism Board at (704) 521–3666.

SALISBURY

Salisbury, the largest city in western North Carolina until the early 1900s, was once a center for trade and politics. Today the city, located southeast of Salisbury at the juncture of Highway 70 and Interstate 85, celebrates its rich heritage with eight separate historic districts where you can take a walk back in time. When you get to Salisbury, head to the Visitors Information Center, located downtown in a restored train station at 215 Depot Street. Here you can pick up a brochure or free audiotapes for the **Salisbury**

Heritage Tour and the Salisbury National Cemetery Tour. The sites
that you won't want to miss while visiting Salisbury are Josephus Hall
House and the 1820 Federal-style home of the chief surgeon of the Salisbury Confederate Prison. A Civil War cannon rests on the lawn in front of
the home, which has been renovated with Greek and Victorian touches.
Tours by costumed guides are given on weekends. Another interesting
home is the Old Stone House, an impressive two-story stone structure
built in 1766. On the second story you'll find two openings believed to be
gunports used to fight off hostile Indians. The Salisbury Visitor's Information Center is open from 9:00 A.M. to 5:00 P.M. Monday through Friday,
10:00 A.M. to 4:00 P.M. Saturday, and 1:00 to 4:00 P.M. Sunday. Call (800)
332–2343 for more information.

SPENCER

Just north of Salisbury on Highway 70 is the town of Spencer. Everything
you want to know about transportation you can learn at the North Carolina Transportation Museum at Historic Spencer Shops, located on
South Salisbury Avenue. The Spencer Shops were once the largest steam
locomotive servicing station operated by the Southern Railway. Built in
1896 and now a State Historic Site, it features exhibits on the development
of vehicles, from the dugout canoe to the airplane. You can also see vintage
automobiles and take a train ride through the 30-acre facility. Admission to
the museum is free. From April through October, the museum is open
from 9:00 A.M. to 5:00 P.M. Monday through Saturday and 1:00 to 5:00
P.M. Sunday. November through March hours are 10:00 A.M. to 4:00 P.M.
Tuesday through Saturday and 1:00 to 4:00 P.M. Sunday. Call (704)
636–2889 for more information.

THOMASVILLE

You might not plan an entire vacation around the town of Thomasville, but
it is a beautiful, charming town to pass through. It's east of Spencer, just off
Interstate 85. Thomasville's symbol is the World's Largest Chair. You
will know you are in furniture country when you stop at the town square
to see the 30-foot-high wood-framed chair that rests majestically on a granite pedestal. In addition, the town is home of the oldest remaining railroad

depot in the state, also located in the town square. Next, head north on
Interstate 85 and you'll find a rest stop that makes a great place for a picnic
and a chance to see the **North Carolina Vietnam Veterans Memorial.**
Located down a short trail, the memorial features crepe myrtles and brick
walls in honor of the 216,000 North Carolinians who served in Vietnam
and the 1,600 who died or are missing. Call the Thomasville Tourism
Commission at (800) 611–9907 for more information.

HIGH POINT

High Point, north of Thomasville off Interstate 85 or Highway 70, is North
Carolina's main furniture manufacturing center, with 125 furniture manufacturing plants. It is also the home of the **Furniture Discovery Center** at
101 West Green Drive. A colorful museum, it takes you through the
furniture-making process in an interesting way, from lumber milling to
detailed carving. The museum is laid out in color-coded stations that let
you get hands-on experience with tools used in furniture making, including
an air-powered nail gun and a paint-spray gun (Plexiglass keeps little fingers
safe). In addition, you can see several miniature collections. The gift shop
at the museum has a wide selection of books on furniture making as well
as crafts. Museum admission costs $3.50 for adults, $3.00 for students sixteen and up, and $1.50 for children six to fifteen years of age. The furni-
ture center is open from 10:00 A.M. to 5:00 P.M. Tuesday through Saturday
and 1:00 to 5:00 P.M. Sunday. The center is also open on Mondays from
April through October. Call (910) 887–3876 for more information.

Anyone who's ever played with dolls will love the **Angela Peterson
Doll and Miniature Museum,** adjacent to the furniture center. Here you
will find one of the greatest collections of dolls anywhere. It features more
than 1,600 dolls, miniatures, and artifacts from around the world. This
exquisite collection took more than fifty years of travel to put together, and
Angela Peterson, who is now in her eighties, made many of the costumes,
shadow boxes, and dollhouses herself. As you enter the main gallery you'll
see dozens of glass cases filled with china dolls, along with dolls made of
papier-mâché, wax, and tin, some dating back to the 1800s. Fans of royalty
will get a kick out of seeing Princess Diana in her wedding dress. A 3-foot-
high Shirley Temple doll may prompt some stories from Grandma. Among

the most interesting in the collection are an unusual doll made of seaweed and the dressed fleas you have to look at under a magnifier. And don't forget the more modern collection of Barbie dolls and the Pillsbury Doughboy. Admission costs $3.00 for adults, $1.50 for students over fifteen, and 50 cents for children six to fifteen years of age. Museum hours are 10:00 A.M. to 5:00 P.M. Tuesday through Saturday and 1:00 to 5:00 P.M. Sunday. The museum is also open on Mondays from April through October. Call (910) 885–3655 for more information.

You can get a guide to High Point's historical attractions by contacting the High Point Convention and Visitors Bureau (910–884–5255), and you'll want to make sure you see the **High Point Museum and Historical Park,** at Lexington and McGuinn drives. The museum contains woodworking tools dating back to the nineteenth century as well as local artifacts and Civil War items. Also on the grounds is John Haley House, an early brick Quaker house, the oldest structure still standing in Guilford County. Built in 1786, the house has been fully restored, and the grounds also include a weaving house and blacksmith shop. Admission is free. The museum, house, and grounds are open from 10:00 A.M. to 4:30 P.M. Tuesday through Saturday and 1:00 to 4:30 P.M. Sunday. Call (910) 885–6859 for more information.

One of the newcomers on the family fun scene in High Point is the **Carolina Dynamo,** a soccer team that springs into action each April at A. J. Simmeon Stadium at the High Point Athletic Complex. Each home game brings an array of promotional events, including a fans' kick for $15,000 toward the purchase of a new car and a kids' competition for soccer gear. D. D., the 8-foot soccer dog, comes out of his house in the 10,000-seat stadium to give away premium items. Tickets for games cost $6.00 for adults, $5.00 for students twelve through twenty-one, $4.00 for kids two through twelve, and are free for children under two. Call (910) 852–9969 for more information.

WINSTON-SALEM

North of High Point, via State Highway 109 near Interstate 40, is Winston-Salem. While there are a number of hotels and other accommodations in the area, the most popular place to stay is **Tanglewood Park,** a

Travel back in time at Old Salem, an eighteenth-century Moravian village. (Courtesy Winston-Salem Convention and Visitors Bureau)

great outdoor recreational facility, about ten minutes from downtown Winston-Salem. It offers a bed-and-breakfast inn in an old manor house as well as cottages and a neat campground. The park offers 1,100 acres for golf, tennis, swimming, horseback riding, hiking, studying nature, and fishing. Included are two top-rate golf courses and a par-three course for families who just want to get out on the course for a couple hours. You'll also find miniature golf and horse stables as well. The park is open for daytime activities from 7:00 A.M. to dusk. Call (910) 766–0591 for more information. For information on other accommodations in the area call (800) 331–7018.

Winston-Salem's most popular attraction is **Old Salem,** a living-history eighteenth-century Moravian village that takes you back in time. You'll want to spend most of the day here as costumed guides take you through the community from which the city evolved. More than eighty structures, dating back to 1766, have been fully restored. The most popular among kids is Winkler Bakery, where fresh sugar cakes, gingerbread cookies, and other tasty goodies are made using early methods and recipes. You can also see the Boys School; John Vogley House, which includes a collection of nineteenth-century toys; a structure that served as a meat market and firehouse; Shultz shop, the shoemaker's shop; and more. A film on Moravian life is also presented in a theater inside Vierling Barn. In addition, you can take a half-hour carriage ride on the cobblestone streets of the district. Admission costs $14.00 for adults and $8.00 for children ages six to sixteen. A carriage ride runs about $20.00. Old Salem is open from 9:30 A.M. to 4:30 P.M. Monday through Saturday and 1:30 to 4:30 P.M. Sunday. Call (800) 441–5305 for more information.

More history awaits you at **Historic Bethabara Park,** located north of town off University Parkway. It's a great place for outdoor activities, to have a picnic, or to stroll along the walking trails, but history is alive here, too. You can visit Palisade Fort, originally built in 1756 during the French and Indian War and reconstructed on its original site. You'll also find the 1788 Gemeinhuas, a church; a 1782 Potter's House; and an 1803 Brewer's House. Admission is free. You can tour the buildings from 9:30 A.M. to 4:30 P.M. Monday through Friday and 1:30 to 4:30 P.M. Saturday and Sunday. Call (910) 924–8191 for more information.

For those who like to meet people from around the world, check out the **Museum of Anthropology,** located on the campus of Wake Forest University. This is the only museum of its kind in the southeast. The museum is dedicated to the study of world cultures and includes exhibits related to these studies. Featured are costumes, clothing, tools, and more related to human development around the world. It also relates some of the greater achievements of the people from the Americas, Africa, Asia, and the Pacific. Admission is free. It is open from 10:00 A.M. to 4:30 P.M. Tuesday through Saturday. Call (910) 759–5282 for more information.

Three centuries of American art are on display at **Reynolda House Museum of American Art,** located off Reynolda Road near the university. The museum is located on the country estate and model farm built by tobacco magnate R. J. Reynolds and his wife, Katherine Smith Reynolds. The house, built in 1917, is filled with beautiful paintings, prints, sculptures, and furnishings, some of which date back to the seventeenth century. Also included is a ladies' costume collection that dates back to nearly 1900. Japanese cherry trees on the grounds bloom to magnificent color in late March. Admission to the museum costs $6.00 for adults and $3.00 for students through age seventeen. Admission to the gardens is free. The house is open from 9:30 A.M. to 4:30 P.M. Tuesday through Saturday and 1:30 to 4:30 P.M. Sunday. It is closed Thanksgiving, Christmas, and New Year's Day. Call (910) 725–5325 for more information.

Science lovers will get their fill in Winston-Salem, too. **SciWorks,** 400 West Hanes Mill Road, is a 45,000-square-foot science center and environmental park that lets kids and adults alike uncover some of the mysteries of science. Here you can actually do experiments yourself, while staff members put on displays designed to astonish you. You can learn more about the sea at the aquariums, at the touch tank, and through CD-ROM computer programs of undersea adventure. The center also includes a 120-seat planetarium that presents various shows year-round. In addition, you can take a walk or have a picnic in the 34-acre park. Here you're likely to come face-to-face with a deer or river otter, and the kids get a chance to meet farmyard animals. Admission costs $4.00 for adults, $3.00 for young people six to nineteen, and $1.00 for children ages three to five. The center and park are open 10:00 A.M. to 5:00 P.M. Monday through

Saturday and 1:00 to 5:00 P.M. Sunday. Call (910) 767–6730 for more information.

More adventure awaits you at the **Southeastern Center for Contemporary Arts,** located in the English-style manor house of the late industrialist James G. Hanes at 750 Marguerite Drive. Although this is the center for arts in the southeast, you can enjoy fascinating works from around the world in changing exhibits from well-known artists. In addition, the museum presents occasional interpretive programs on exhibits as well as performing arts programs. Also, a wide array of contemporary crafts are on display at the Centershop. Admission costs $3.00 for anyone age thirteen or older and is free for children age twelve or younger. The center is open from 10:00 A.M. to 5:00 P.M. Tuesday through Saturday and 2:00 to 5:00 P.M. Sunday. Call (910) 725–1904 for more information.

MOUNT AIRY

If you're staying in the triad area—Winston-Salem, High Point, or Greensboro—a great day trip is less than an hour northwest on U.S. Highway 52, where you'll find Mount Airy. The town was made famous as the model for Mayberry in the popular television series *The Andy Griffith Show.* Griffith, the show's star (who later became the title character in television's *Matlock*), was born and raised here until he left to attend college in Chapel Hill. His house and the **Andy Griffith Playhouse** have been preserved as landmarks and are on the town's tour of historical places. Memorabilia from the show and Griffith's career can be found throughout the town. In addition, the playhouse is the venue for productions throughout the year. Call the town visitor center at (800) 576–0231 for more information on Mount Airy.

To the south and west of Mount Airy you will find two state parks that are great for recreational activities. **Hanging Rock State Park** (910–593–8480), located off Highway 89, provides a great opportunity for picnicking, hiking, camping, and swimming. An interesting granite formation pokes out of the earth at **Pilot Mountain State Park** (910–325–2355), located off Highway 52. Here a number of recreational activities are available in addition to a family campground. Both parks are open from sunrise to sunset daily, year-round. Admission is free.

GREENSBORO

With a population of nearly 200,000, Greensboro regularly rates as one of the nation's most desirable places in the country to live. Located in the heart of the Northern Piedmont, it is North Carolina's third largest city and is easily accessible by Interstates 85 and 40. The Piedmont Triad International Airport has made it one of the Southeast's more economically successful business centers, with businesses ranging from textiles to tobacco to service-related industries, such as insurance. For the visitor it hosts a wide variety of activities that include outdoor sports, such as golf and tennis, as well as spectator sports that include Atlantic Coast Conference Basketball action, class A baseball, and professional hockey. Greensboro is a center for arts, history and culture as well. For more information on Greensboro and its accommodations, call the Greensboro Convention and Visitors Bureau at (800) 344–2282.

Much of Greensboro's roots are tied up at one of the city's most popular attractions, the **Guilford County Courthouse National Military Park,** located on Battleground Avenue (Highway 22). It is the country's first Revolutionary War park and features more than 200 acres of wooded trails, monuments, and memorials. It memorializes a bloody battle at Guilford Courthouse, then the county seat, that occurred in March 1781. In that battle American Major General Nathaniel Greene, for whom the city is named, lost control of the area to the British but in the process took out more than a quarter of their troops. The British soon lost North Carolina as a result. The entire battle is re-created at the visitor center through an audiovisual display and exhibits of period artifacts. Admission is free. The park is open from 8:30 A.M. to 5:00 P.M. daily.

You can learn more about the state's history from the Revolutionary War period to the early 1800s at **Tannenbaum Park,** 103 Green Acres Lane, near the National Military Park. At the heart of the park is **Hoskins House** (circa 1778). It is nearly 45 percent original but has been restored to what historians believe to be its original condition. Occasional living history programs bring the house—including the kitchen, barn, and blacksmith shop—alive with demonstrations from interpreters. The Colonial Backcountry farm is host to field crop and gardening exhibits and presentations. The **North Carolina Colonial Heritage Center** at the park provides an opportunity for hands-on participation in learning about backcountry life. Here vistors can try on colonial clothes, feel the weight of a real musket, and see up close how colonial people made their clothes and furnishings. Admission is free. The heritage center is open from 9:00 A.M. to 5:00 P.M. Tuesday through Friday, 10:00 A.M. to 5:00 P.M. Saturday, and 1:00 to 5:00 P.M. Sunday. Call (910) 288–8259 for information on the center or a schedule of living history events at Hoskins House.

Much more history about the Greensboro area is waiting for you at the **Greensboro Historical Museum,** 130 Summit Avenue, where you get a glimpse into the lives of some of the area's more prominent residents. Among them is Greensboro native William Sidney Porter, who gave his account of the city's occupation by Union troops in the stories he wrote under the name O. Henry. Other displays highlight the lives of First Lady Dolly Madison and famed television journalist Edward R. Murrow. The museum, housed in a Romanesque church built in 1892, also features changing exhibits and displays on early transportation, military history, and Native American settlements. You can also learn about the famous sit-in at the Woolworth lunch counter in 1960 that helped launch the national civil rights movement. Admission is free. The museum is open 10:00 A.M. to 5:00 P.M. Tuesday through Saturday and 2:00 to 5:00 P.M. Sunday. Call (910) 373–2043 for more information.

Historical elegance is only a short drive away at **Blandwood Mansion and Carriage House,** a nineteenth-century Italian villa located at 447 West Washington Street. The house, originally built as a farmhouse in the late eighteenth century, was redesigned and totally renovated in 1844. Blandwood served as home for former North Carolina Governor and Whig party politician John Motley Morehead and today still contains many of its original furnishings. The adjacent carriage house serves as the site for many formal receptions and meetings. A small admission fee is charged to tour the house, which is open during limited hours. Call (910) 272–5003 for more information.

Greensboro's history continues into the twentieth century at the **Charlotte Hawkins Brown State Historic Site,** located northeast of Greensboro off Interstate 85. North Carolina's first official site to honor an African American and a woman, it is the former location of the Palmer

Institute, a black prep school that Brown founded in 1902 when she was only nineteen years old. Eventually the school grew to 350 acres, included a farm, and received full accreditation by the Southern Association of Colleges and Secondary Schools. Today you can see displays about the school, Brown's life, and the civil rights movement. Also included are her home and gravesite. Admission is free. During the summer the site is open from 9:00 A.M. to 5:00 P.M. Monday through Saturday and 1:00 to 5:00 P.M. Sunday. Winter hours are 10:00 A.M. to 4:00 P.M. Tuesday through Friday and 1:00 to 4:00 P.M. Sunday. Call (910) 449–4846 for more information.

You'll find Greensboro's arts downtown at the **Greensboro Cultural Center.** The center features five galleries that include different types and themes in the visual arts. The African American Atelier (910–333–6885) exhibits original artwork by local African-American artists and provides educational programs to the community's youth. The Green Hill Center for North Carolina Art (910–333–7460) features changing exhibits and programs that include works in glass, ceramics, jewelry, and painting. The Greensboro Artists' League Gallery and Gift Shop (910–333–7485) includes a sales gallery as well as changing exhibits of the works of artists in the Triad area. The Guilford Native American Art Gallery (910–273–6605) has contemporary Native American arts and crafts on display and for sale. The Mattye Reed African American Heritage Center (910–334–7108) is a satellite center located on the campus of North Carolina A&T State University. This museum has a seemingly unending collection of African culture exhibits from more than thirty African nations, New Guinea, and Haiti. Admission to all the museums and galleries is free, but hours vary. Call each museum for hours of operation or other details.

Three of the state's most beautiful and intriguing botanical gardens are located in Greensboro. The **Bog Garden,** located on Hobbs Road, provides an interesting twist to this swampy land. The marsh has been transformed into a beautiful area that includes more than 8,000 trees, shrubs, ferns, bamboo, and wildflowers. A wooden walkway takes you through the bog, where plants are labeled for visitors' education. **Bicentennial Gardens,** completed in 1976 to commemorate the nation's bicentennial and located off Highway 29 North, features spectacular rose gardens as well as a fragrance and herb garden. It's hard to find a time of year when this garden won't bring you color. A favorite among kids is the **Greensboro Arboretum,** located on Wendover Avenue, which features 17 acres of gardens, including a butterfly garden and eight other labeled plant collections. No admission is charged at any of the gardens. They are open from 8:00 A.M. to sunset daily. Call (910) 373–2558 for more information.

Greensboro has much to offer sports lovers. **Forest Oaks Country Club** (800–999–5446), located on Highway 421 South, is the site of the Kmart Greater Greensboro Open, one of the five richest golf tournaments on the PGA tour. Well-known golf stars come out for this event each April to compete for the $1.5 million purse.

In addition to pro golf, the **Greensboro Coliseum Complex** (910–373–7474), located at 1921 West Lee Street, is the site of a number of college events as well as the occasional host to the Atlantic Coast Conference basketball tournament. The coliseum is also the home for the Carolina Monarchs, a professional ice hockey team. The coliseum additionally hosts such nonsporting events as Ringling Brothers Circus, trade shows, flea markets, and more.

War Memorial Stadium (910–333–2287), located at the corner of Lindsay and Yanceyville streets, is home of the Carolina Bats, a Class A farm team for the New York Yankees. The Bats have special promotions practically every game night. These include giving away hats, pennants, and other novelties on a regular basis. They also have special picnic packages that combine your dinner with a seat at the game. Check the local media for the dates of special dollar nights to attend a game in the 7,000-seat stadium at a bargain price. Tickets to the game start at $4.00, while picnic packages begin at $8.00.

Those who want to get in on some action themselves and cool off during the warm summer months can head to **Emerald Pointe Water Park,** located just off Interstate 85 on South Holden Road. Splash and play here at the Carolinas' largest water park, which offers twenty-two water rides and attractions, in addition to an exciting Sky Coaster ride that lets you fly suspended under a giant arch. One admission price of $16.50 lets you enjoy a full day of playing in the water, in the waves, and on the slides that are made for both the big and the small. After 4:00 P.M. you can get in for $11.00. Children less than 45 inches tall get a $4.00 discount and are restricted to certain attractions The Sky Coaster requires an additional charge. Hours vary according to season and weather. Call (800) 555–5900 for more information.

You'll find more than water fun at **Celebration Station,** a great family entertainment center located at 4315 Big Tree Way just off Interstate 40. The park includes miniature golf, bumper boats, go-carts, batting cages, arcade games, a pizza restaurant, and a snack bar where you can grab a foot-long hot dog or a salad. The center is set up so each age group has its own area, making the activities safe for young children as well as their older siblings. It's also a lot of fun, especially if you have toddlers, to order a pizza and listen to the entertainment from the Dixie Diggers, an animated musical band of animals. Each ride or miniature golf game costs $3.50, or you can purchase a ticket for unlimited rides for $13.99 per person. It is open from 10:00 A.M. to 10:00 P.M. Monday through Thursday and 10:00 A.M. to 11:00 P.M. Friday and Saturday. Call (910) 316–0606 for more information.

You can probably make a day out of a visit to the **Natural Science Center of Greensboro,** 4301 Lawndale Drive. It's a real treat to visit this hands-on museum, zoo, and planetarium. If your kids like dinosaurs, and they probably do, they'll love visiting the fine dinosaur gallery as much as they'll like the snakes and amphibians at the herpetarium. Here and at the touch labs, they'll learn a lot about minerals and gems. The kids can meet animals up close at the petting zoo, where they will find donkeys, rabbits, goats, and more. They can also see a black bear and a jaguar at the zoo, but they can't pet them. The **Edward R. Zane Planetarium** is always ready to show an entertaining and educational show under its own stars. The science center is open from 9:00 A.M. to 5:00 P.M. Monday through Saturday and 12:30 to 5:00 P.M. Sunday. Admission to the center costs $5.50 for adults and $4.50 for children ages four through thirteen.

Afterward you can spend the afternoon at **Country Park,** adjacent to the science center. The park offers fishing at two stocked lakes, paddleboats, playgrounds, fields for running and playing, and trails for hiking and jogging. It's also a great place for a picnic. The park is open from 8:00 A.M. to sunset daily.

REIDSVILLE

Head North from Greensboro on Highway 29 and you'll find the town of Reidsville, home of one of the prettiest plantations in the state. **Chinqua-Penn Plantation,** located on Wentworth Street, is the beautifully preserved home of Thomas Jefferson Penn. The twenty-seven room mansion, built in 1925, reflects the exciting lifestyle of Penn and his wife and is filled with an extensive collection of artwork and furnishings from Russia, Egypt, China, and France. Some pieces date as far back as 1100 B.C. Outside, the gardens reflect the same exquisite taste, from the fountains to the pagoda gardens. Admission costs $7.00 for adults and $2.50 for anyone age seventeen or younger. The plantation is open from March through December from 10:00 A.M. to 6:00 P.M. Tuesday through Saturday and 1:00 to 6:00 P.M. Sunday. Call (910) 349–4576 for more information.

JAMESTOWN

Mendehall Plantation, located 2 miles southwest of Greensboro at 603 West Main Street in the town of Jamestown, is an early nineteenth-century Quaker plantation. It consists of a number of interesting structures, a museum, and one of only two false-bottom wagons still in existence. The wagon was used to transport escaped slaves during the operation of the Underground Railroad. Admission is free, but donations are accepted. The plantation is open for tours from April through the third week in December from 11:00 A.M. to 2:00 P.M. Tuesday through Friday and 1:00 to 4:00 P.M. Saturday. Call (910) 454–3819 for more information.

LEVEL CROSS

Greensboro's central location makes for a number of ideal day trips, particularly to the south, where you'll find the town of Level Cross and the **Richard Petty Museum.** Located off Highway 220 south, the museum is a tribute to the king of NASCAR racing. Petty won seven Winston Cup Championships during his career, and today the museum, located in his hometown, houses a fine collection of memorabilia commemorating his career. Included are a number of cars he raced, his trophies, and tons of other awards and recognitions he received. You can also see on video some of the most exciting moments of his career in addition to photos that include his crash at Daytona Speedway. Admission to the museum costs $3.00 for adults and $1.50 for students and is free for children age six or younger. Call (910) 495–1143 for more information.

ASHEBORO

Continue south on Highway 220 to reach Asheboro. Here you'll want to head to one of the best family attractions in the state, the **North Carolina Zoo,** one of the largest walk-through zoos in the world. You won't have any trouble finding the zoo; signs lead you right to it from Highway 220 or Highway 49/64. Great care has been taken to create this natural-habitat zoo to give you the best possible view of the animals on display. While you can walk through the zoo, a tram allows you to go back and see your favorite parts over and over. The North American Region, with more than 200 acres, features ten different exhibits that cover everything from deserts to swamps to prairies. In this region you'll see bison, road-runners, rattlesnakes, and polar bears diving into a huge tank of water. In addition, the kids will want to visit the Touch and Learn Center where they can pet a Shetland pony, sheep, goats, and more. Also part of the North American Region is the Red Wolf Species Survival Plan, one ele-ment of the zoo's commitment to save the endangered animal and rein-troduce it into the wild.

Next, journey to Africa at the zoo's 300-acre region that includes nine exhibits with the biggest animals you've ever seen. Here antelope graze an open plain, giraffes tower at tree-top level, and elephants come up close and personal. In this region you also get a chance to look mas-sive gorillas in the eye and muse at the antics of monkeys and baboons. One of the best parts of the African Region is the R. J. Reynolds Forest Aviary. It is an enclosed miniature jungle that houses more than 1,700 tropical plants and 100 birds, and they're not in cages. In the aviary you can peer into the bushes to find a kingfisher or see any number of other species flying down from the ceiling. The zoo is open from April through October, 9:00 A.M. to 5:00 P.M. daily and 9:00 A.M. to 4:00 P.M. daily the rest of the year.

Parking is free, and there is a picnic area located at the main entrance, with snack bars and refreshment stands scattered throughout the park. Lockers are also provided. Admission costs $8.00 for adults and $5.00 for children ages two through twelve. Call (800) 488–0444 for more information.

SEAGROVE

Seagrove, south of Asheboro on Highway 220, and the surrounding area could well be the pottery capitol of the world. The **Seagrove Area Potteries** bring to life a tradition that has been passed down through the ages. In this area, you'll find more than seventy potteries where potters work and put their wares on sale. Pottery was first made here by Native Americans in the 1500s; today's works have been refined, thanks to modern technology. Here you can purchase a whole set of dishes or even a pottery bird feeder. The annual **Pottery Festival,** sponsored by the Friends of the Pottery Museum, is held in Seagrove each November on the Sunday before Thanksgiving. In addition to pottery, the crafts of doll making, candle making, wood carving, and more are demonstrated. For more information, call the museum at (910) 873–7887.

BURLINGTON

If you had chosen to head east instead of south from Greensboro, Interstate 40 or Highway 70 would take you to Burlington. The city of Burlington has grown to become a shopping mecca for North Carolina residents, but it offers plenty of history and other attractions for your family to enjoy. The county's textile heritage has led to the creation of **Burlington Manufacturer's Outlet Center,** the largest such center in North Carolina. The shops here sell everything from kidswear to home furnishings, while the downtown shopping district offers a variety of charming specialty and retail shops. The center is open from 10:00 A.M. to 9:00 P.M. Monday through Saturday and 1:00 to 6:00 P.M. Sunday. You can call the Burlington Convention and Visitors Bureau at (800) 637–3804 for more information on shopping in the city.

You can start a historical tour of the Burlington area at the **Alamance Battleground State Historic Site,** located on Highway 62 South off Interstate 85/40. This is the site where Royal Governor William Tryon in 1771 led the North Carolina Militia into a battle against 2,000 Regulators, an

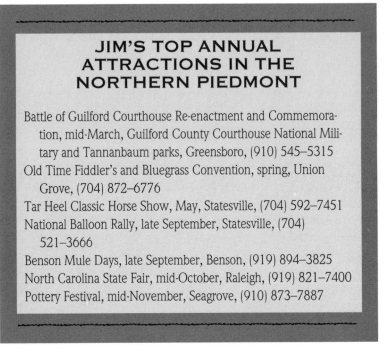

JIM'S TOP ANNUAL ATTRACTIONS IN THE NORTHERN PIEDMONT

Battle of Guilford Courthouse Re-enactment and Commemoration, mid-March, Guilford County Courthouse National Military and Tannanbaum parks, Greensboro, (910) 545–5315

Old Time Fiddler's and Bluegrass Convention, spring, Union Grove, (704) 872–6776

Tar Heel Classic Horse Show, May, Statesville, (704) 592–7451

National Balloon Rally, late September, Statesville, (704) 521–3666

Benson Mule Days, late September, Benson, (919) 894–3825

North Carolina State Fair, mid-October, Raleigh, (919) 821–7400

Pottery Festival, mid-November, Seagrove, (910) 873–7887

army of colonial reformers who protested taxes, corrupt officials, and the lack of representation. You can learn more about the battle and the Regulator movement at the site. The visitor center presents an audiovisual display as well as other historical information. In addition, you can visit the John Allen House, a log home typical of this area in the late 1700s. It has been restored and contains its original furnishings. Admission to the site is free. From April through October it is open from 9:00 A.M. to 5:00 P.M. Monday through Saturday and 1:00 to 5:00 P.M. Sunday. Hours the rest of the year are 9:00 A.M. to 4:00 P.M. Tuesday through Saturday and 1:00 to 4:00 P.M. Sunday. Call (910) 227–4785 for more information.

A great way to spend an afternoon is at **Cedarock Historical Farm,** located off Highway 49 South. This is a unique, 414-acre park that features a rolling terrain full of cedar trees and rock outcroppings, hence its name. Now restored to its original condition, this farm and its buildings were originally constructed in 1830 by John and Polly Garrett. Today a variety of livestock are kept on the farms, including goats, sheep, and cattle, as well as Jed and Jethro, the team of working mules. A museum includes antique farm equipment and demonstrations of long-lost farming techniques. Admission is free. The farm is open from 9:00 A.M. to 4:00 P.M. Wednesday through Friday and 1:00 to 4:00 P.M. Saturday and Sunday. Call (910) 570–6769 for more information.

When you are in Burlington make sure you visit **City Park,** especially if you have young children. This 60-acre park, located at South Church Street and Overbrook Road, offers miniature golf and amusement rides in addition to traditional park facilities, such as picnic tables and a pool. But the centerpiece of the park is a Dentzel Menagerie Carousel made in 1910. This is a beautiful piece of work. The carousel has forty-six hand-carved animals, no two alike. Included are twenty-six horses with real horsehair tails and a variety of other bright animals ranging from pigs to reindeer. Other rides, including a train and boats, are small and great for younger children and even toddlers. Admission for each ride is less than $1.00. The park generally is open during daylight hours. Call (910) 222–5030 for more information.

SNOW CAMP

Although Snow Camp is a small town, it boasts one of the best drama societies in the state. The **Snow Camp Ampitheatre,** located on State Road 1005 south of Burlington, is easy to find. The most popular annual production is *Sword of Peace*, which is presented alternately with *Pathway to Freedom*. Much of Alamance County's history is presented in William Hardy's *Sword of Peace*, a tribute to the Quakers and their role in the American Revolution. In this action-packed production, Simon Miller, a Quaker miller, must decide whether his faith allows him to take part in the Revolution. In *Pathway to Freedom*, playwright Mark R. Sumner tells the fictional story of the son of a slave-owning family and how he became involved with the Underground Railroad. In addition to these wonderful annual productions, Snow Camp also presents other plays that are especially appropriate for children. In the past they have presented such greats as *The Sound of Music*, and Saturday mornings are reserved for young children with productions such as *Cinderella.* Evening shows are presented at 8:30 P.M. from mid-June through late August. Tickets for evening productions cost $8.00 for adults and $5.00 for children age eleven or younger. Tickets to children's theater productions presented at 10:00 A.M. cost $4.00 for all ages. Call (800) 726–5115 for more information.

CHAPEL HILL

Three cities to the east of Burlington and Snow Camp—Raleigh, Durham, and Chapel Hill—lie in a geometric shape known as the Triangle Area. If you visit this area in the winter months, you should be aware that you are in college basketball country. The state's three main universities are located in the Triangle Area, making for a long-standing rivalry among the teams vying for the Atlantic Coast Conference basketball championship. For years it has been one of the state residents' favorite athletic competitions. Chapel Hill is home of the **University of North Carolina,** the nation's first state-supported university, chartered in 1789. This great town is, for all intents and purposes, the university—the town's population of 40,000 is made up of a largely diverse collection of 24,000 students and professors from across the country, making Chapel Hill a uniquely cosmopolitan town. Franklin Street, which forms the northern edge of the university campus, is full of opportunities for a wide variety of shopping and dining, while the campus provides a multitude of cultural and popular attractions. Parking is not available on campus, but you can use one of the municipal lots on Rosemary or Franklin streets. For more information, call the Chapel Hill/Orange County Visitor's Bureau at (919) 968–2062.

The most easily accessible attraction is **Morehead Planetarium.** Located on Franklin Street, it was once used by NASA as a training center for astronauts. Part of the university, the planetarium houses a rare projector that casts nearly 9,000 stars onto the inside of the planetarium's 68-foot dome. In addition to the 350-seat theater, there are a host of related exhibits, art galleries, a science shop, rose gardens, and a huge sundial. Special programs for children are held most every weekend, and shows are presented in the evenings during the week. Touring the planetarium and exhibits is free, but a nominal admission fee is charged for films and other programs. Hours are 12:30 to 5:00 P.M. and 7:00 to 9:45 P.M. Sunday through Friday and 10:00 A.M. to 5:00 P.M. and 7:00 to 9:45 P.M. Saturday. Call (919) 549–6863 for a schedule of shows.

Next, take a stroll through the oak trees that line brick walks of the campus to the **Ackland Art Museum,** located on Columbia Street less than a block from Franklin Street. Here you'll find a wide range of art—paintings, sculptures, drawings, photographs, and furnishings. Works in the museum's permanent collections come from Europe and Asia as well as the United States. Art from the Renaissance to the present is represented as well as North Carolina pottery and folk art. Admission is free. Hours are 10:00 A.M. to 5:00 P.M. Wednesday through Saturday and 1:00 to 5:00 P.M. Sunday. Call (919) 966–5736 for more information.

While there are few other formal exhibits on the 700-acre campus, the campus itself is well manicured and awe-inspiring. A tape-recorded walking tour is available at the visitor center (919–962–1630) at the planetarium. Some of the sights you will see include the Morehead Patterson Bell tower on South Road, south of the art museum, and the **Dean E. Smith Center,** located on Skipper Bowles Drive on the southern part of campus, the home of the Tarheels and named for the longtime men's basketball coach. You'll probably have to have connections or very good luck to get tickets to a game on campus, but the center is host to other special events and concerts. In addition, you can get a glimpse of the university's rich athletic history in the center's Carolina Athletic Memorabilia Room. It features 3,000 square feet of exhibit space for artifacts, highlight tapes, and other souvenirs. The center is open 8:00 A.M. to 5:00 P.M. Monday through Friday. Admission is free if you want to come in and look around when there's no basketball game. Call (919) 922–2296 for more information.

Just off campus is the **North Carolina Botanical Garden,** located on Old Mason Farm Road. It is the largest natural botanical garden in the Southeast and consists of 600 acres of naturally preserved land. There are miles of walking trails and collections of North Carolina and Southeastern plants arranged in habitats in natural settings. Here you will also see carnivorous plants, aquatic plants, and herb gardens. Admission is free. The gardens are open from 8:00 A.M. to 5:00 P.M. seven days a week from mid-March through mid-November and Monday through Friday only the rest of the year. Call (919) 962–0522 for more information.

HILLSBOROUGH

East of Burlington, just south off Highway 70, is the historic town of Hillsborough. Hillsborough is listed on the National Register of Historic Places
and has more than 100 structures from the late eighteenth and nineteenth
centuries that provided a backdrop for a number of events during the Revolutionary War. Most notable is the site of the Constitutional Convention
of 1788, where delegates demanded a Bill of Rights before they would rat-
ify the Constitution. In addition, the town was significant in the Civil War
and served as headquarters for Confederate General Joseph E. Johnston,
who later negotiated terms of the South's surrender with Union General
William T. Sherman.

The **Orange County Historical Museum,** located at 201 North
Churton Street, illustrates much of Hillsborough's past. The museum
depicts history and lifestyles from the time Indians inhabited the Eno River
area through the Civil War. In addition, the upstairs features work from a
different artist every month. Admission is free. The museum is open from
1:30 to 4:30 P.M. Tuesday through Sunday. Call (919) 732–2201 for more
information.

DURHAM

Although Durham is also noted for its athletic heritage at Duke University,
it is just as notable as a "city of medicine." The university opened its medical school in 1930, there are five major hospitals and a number of pharma-
ceutical research companies, and the city is largely connected to Research
Triangle Park, said to be the world's largest university-related research
park. For more information, call the Durham Convention and Visitors
Bureau at (919) 687–0288.

At Duke University you'll find a number of interesting attractions, most
notable of which is **Duke University Chapel,** located on Chapel Drive in
the west portion of campus. This 1,800-seat chapel was the last of the great
collegiate Gothic projects. It features a 5,033-pipe organ with five keyboards
and a fifty-bell carillon. Its intricate stained-glass windows are also notewor-
thy. No admission is charged to tour the church from 9:00 A.M. to 5:00 P.M.
Monday through Saturday, and nondenominational worship services are
held at 11:00 A.M. Sunday. Call (919) 681–1704 for more information.

Also in the west campus is **Sarah P. Duke Gardens,** located on Anderson Street. Here you find fifty-five acres of beautifully kept gardens, both natural and landscaped. There are more than 1,500 kinds of plants along the paths. The walks feature pathways with bridges, grottoes, court lawns, waterfalls, and pavilions. Such a wide variety of plants exists here that you'll find color in bloom practically all year long. In addition, there is an Asiatic Arboretum. Admission is free. Hours are 9:00 A.M. to 5:00 P.M. Monday through Saturday and 1:00 to 5:00 P.M. Sunday. Call (919) 684–3698 for more information.

The **Duke University Museum of Art,** located on Campus Drive in the east campus, is most notable for its fine collection of medieval sculpture, but it is also host to a lovely collection of stained glass and an extensive collection of pre-Columbian exhibits. The museum's Chinese jade is quite unusual. American and European paintings, prints, and drawings round out the trip to the museum. Admission is free. Hours are 9:00 A.M. to 5:00 P.M. Tuesday through Friday, 11:00 A.M. to 2:00 P.M. Saturday, and 2:00 to 5:00 P.M. Sunday. Call (919) 684–5135 for more information.

Like most major cities in the state, Durham isn't without a rich history. It was at **Bennett Place State Historic Site,** located off Highway 70, that the Civil War ended. Union General William T. Sherman and Confederate General Joseph E. Johnston met at this farmstead in 1865, seventeen days after Confederate General Robert E. Lee surrendered at Appomatox. Following meetings in Hillsborough, the Durham meeting set up the largest surrender of the war. Although fighting continued in the west, this was the conclusion to the bloody War Between the States. Today the farmhouse and outbuildings have been restored, and the grounds also include a museum and interpretive center. Exhibits concentrate on North Carolina's role in the war, and uniforms, flags, and weapons are on display. A surrender re-enactment is presented each April. Admission is free. The site is open from 9:00 A.M. to 5:00 P.M. Monday through Saturday and 1:00 to 5:00 P.M. Sunday. Call (919) 383–4345 for more information.

Long before Durham was a medical center, its roots were deeply embedded in the tobacco industry. Much of this history is available for viewing at the **Duke Homestead State Historic Site and Tobacco Museum.** Located off Interstate 85 and Guess Road, the site includes the

Duke home, constructed in 1852, plus tobacco barns and two early tobacco factories. The museum chronicles the history of the tobacco industry, production, and cigarette manufacturing. A moving mannequin plants tobacco and helps bring the industry into perspective. Admission is free. The site is open from 9:00 A.M. to 5:00 P.M. Monday through Saturday and 1:00 to 5:00 P.M. Sunday. Call (919) 477–5498 for more information.

Of a more modern ilk is the **North Carolina Museum of Life and Science,** 433 Murray Avenue. This is a great interactive museum that features a range of exhibits from railroads to aerospace. Included is a display of the Apollo 15 and Enos, the first U.S. spacecraft to orbit the earth. The museum's nature center is the best part of the museum. Here visitors can see a variety of wildlife and learn more about it through hands-on activities. For example, the kids can hold a box turtle or hear a rabbit's snappy heartbeat. There is a farmyard where the kids can pet the animals. Admission costs $5.00 for adults and $3.50 for children ages three through eleven. The center is open from 9:00 A.M. to 5:00 P.M. Monday through Saturday and 1:00 to 5:00 P.M. Sunday. Call (919) 220–5429 for more information.

One of the most popular attractions for Durham residents happens at the **Durham Bulls Athletic Park,** the home of the Durham Bulls, a Class A baseball affiliate of the Atlanta Braves. The Bulls received national attention in 1987 with the release of the movie *Bull Durham*, starring Susan Sarandon, Kevin Costner, and Tim Robbins. Even before the release of the film, area residents helped set attendance records at what is North Carolina's most famous baseball team's stadium. The park is located at 409 Blackwell Street. Bulls general admission and lawn seat tickets cost $4.50, and box seats cost $6.50. The season mirrors the major league season of April through September. Call (919) 687–6500 for more information.

Whether a baseball game is on your itinerary or not, you can spend an evening at one of several small amusement parks that Durham has to offer. **Wheels Family Fun Park,** located at 715 Hoover Road, is the largest, with more than eight acres of fun and adventure. The park features the basic amusement park facilities, such as bumper cars, go-carts, and video games, but there are also a skating rink and a miniature golf course. Wheels is open from 9:00 A.M. to 9:30 P.M. daily. Rides cost $3.75 each, and skating and miniature golf cost $4.00 each. Call (919) 598–1944 for more information.

RALEIGH

Raleigh, the state capital, with a population of 240,000, has been voted the best place in America to live by both *Fortune* and *Money* magazines. It's just as good a place to visit. Interstate 40 brings you in from the east or west, merging into the handy ring road, Interstate 440, which encircles the city. Raleigh offers all the expected amenities of a big city—the arts, culture, and entertainment—and it abounds with great museums and other educational opportunities at the state's largest university and at the governmental complex. What's more, is that there is plenty of good old-fashioned southern hospitality. The city was founded in 1792 and named for Sir Walter Raleigh, who is credited with founding the first English Colonies in the Carolinas. While there are big buildings and lots of traffic, one of the first things you'll notice is the abundance of oak trees that add to the city's charm. For general information on Raleigh and information on accommodations, contact the Greater Raleigh Convention and Visitors Bureau at (800) 849–8499.

A good place to start your visit to Raleigh is downtown. In addition to the state government complex, you'll find museums and more. The **State Capitol** (919–733–4994) is located in the geographic center of downtown. Built in the late 1830s in a Greek Revival style, it houses the governor's office, cabinet offices, legislative chambers, and the state library. The state **Legislative Building** (919–733–7928) is located across Bicentennial Plaza and is home to the North Carolina General Assembly. Devoted solely to the legislative branch, visitors get an opportunity to view the legislative process when the General Assembly is in session. Both buildings are open from 8:00 A.M. to 5:00 P.M. Monday through Friday, 9:00 A.M. to 5:00 P.M. Saturday, and 1:00 to 5:00 P.M. Sunday. Admission is free.

Next, check out the **North Carolina Museum of Natural Sciences,** located on the Bicentennial Plaza. It's a small but fine museum that includes live animals in interactive displays that depict the state's natural history. Most impressive is the collection of marine animals. At Whale Hall you find a whale skeleton, mounted dolphins, and whaling tools from the nineteenth century. You'll also see exhibits of native birds and animals in their modeled natural settings. At the Fossil Lab you are likely to find workers explaining the archeology process. A $1.00 donation is suggested for admission. The museum is open 9:00 A.M. to 5:00 P.M. Monday through Saturday and 1:00 to 5:00 P.M. Sunday. Call (919) 733–7450 for more information.

Not far away, at 1 East Edenton Street, you'll find the **North Carolina Museum of History.** The museum is divided into four different sections, each depicting a part of North Carolina's history. Included are displays that give you a chronological history, women's role in the state's history, folklife, and sports. Artifacts tell North Carolina's story from the earliest settlements on Roanoke Island as well as the state's role in the Revolutionary and Civil wars. Admission is free. The museum is open from 9:00 A.M. to 5:00 P.M. Tuesday through Saturday and 1:00 to 6:00 P.M. Sunday. Call (919) 715–0200 for more information.

You can take a short walk from the museum east on Jones Street to 200 North Blount Street to see the **Executive Mansion.** An impressive mansion built in the Victorian style of architecture, it was constructed largely of handmade bricks and has housed twenty-five families since its completion in 1891. Self-guided tours of the home are permitted on an irregular basis. The Capital Area Visitors Center, located nearby, also conducts guided tours with advance notice. Call (919) 733–3456 for hours or other information.

The visitor center also offers walking tours of these attractions and historic homes in the area on Sundays at 2:00 P.M., but you're also welcome to set out on your own. The **Historic Oakwood** neighborhood (919–834–0887) is a 20-block area of Victorian homes built in the late 1800s, bordered by Delson, Edenton, Boundary, and Watauga streets. Just west of downtown on Hargett Street is the **Joel Lane House** (919–833–3431), which was built in the 1760s and is Raleigh's oldest dwelling. In 1782, representatives of the newly formed legislature selected this site as the capital and purchased 1,000 acres of the Lane plantation to create the city of Raleigh. The furnishings in the home are authentic to the period. Just north of downtown at 1 Mimosa Street you will find **Mordecai Historic Park** (919–834–4844), a former antebellum plantation. Here you can get a glimpse of nineteenth-century life and see the cabin where Andrew Johnson, the nation's seventeenth president, was born. Admission to tour the Lane House and Oakwood is free, but the Mordecai tour costs $3.00 per person. Oakwood can be toured at any time. The Lane House is open on an irregular basis, and the Mordecai Park is open from 10:00 A.M. to 3:00 P.M. Monday through Friday and from 1:30 to 3:30 P.M. Saturday and Sunday.

One of the best stops downtown for kids is **Playspace,** a museum that teaches through creative activites and just plain fun. Located at 208 Wolfe Street, it's a place designed for families with small children. A special section for infants and toddlers provides an opportunity for Mom and Dad to play, too. For older children, you'll find a water table and a climbing castle. They can learn about the adult world at the child-sized town that includes a grocery store, bank, restaurant, and more. A favorite at the museum is the puppet theater. Shows begin on the hour and last fifty minutes. Admission costs $1.50 per person, all ages. Free family days are the last Sunday in March, April, September, and October. Playspace is open from 9:00 A.M. to 1:00 P.M. Monday and 9:00 A.M. to 5:00 P.M. Tuesday through Saturday. Call (919) 832–1212 for more information.

When you leave downtown, take Hillsborough Street to **North Carolina State University,** the state's largest institute of higher learning, with 27,000 students. The university is almost a completely separate town. The campus, noted for its red brick walkways and buildings, is host to Wolfpack basketball, football, and other sports. In addition it provides venues for concerts, theater, and the arts. Among the attractions you'll find here are the NCSU **Solar House** (919–515–3799), a solar demonstration house constructed at Western Boulevard and Gorman Street by the College of Engineering. The Solar House is open from 9:00 A.M. to 5:00 P.M. Monday through Friday and 1:00 to 5:00 P.M. Sunday. Admission is free. Another attraction you won't want to miss is the NCSU Arboretum (919–515–7641), which features 6,000 different kinds of plants from fifty-five countries. Located off Old Hillsborough Street at 4301 Beryl Road, the arboretum also includes a Victorian gazebo and a Japanese garden, with guided tours at 2:00 P.M. Sunday from mid-April to mid-October. Admission is free.

The best time to visit Raleigh is in the fall when the **North Carolina State Fairgrounds,** on Blue Ridge Road near the university, come alive with the excitement of the annual state fair. The fair is a traditional festival featuring rides, games, and farm-related events and exhibitions. It is usually held for ten days in the middle of October. When the fair isn't in town, the grounds are host to a flea market on the weekends and a variety of other shows, including livestock and pet shows. Rodeos are also periodically held here, and the fairgrounds are the Raleigh venue for the Ringling Brothers, Barnum and Bailey Circus. Call (919) 821–7400 for more information.

North of the university on Blue Ridge Road is the **North Carolina Museum of Art.** It houses the permanent art collection of the state as well as changing exhibits. The museum contains paintings and sculptures dating back 5,000 years and come from as far away as Egypt. Included are works by Raphael, Monet, Botticelli, and others. Guided tours are conducted at 1:30 P.M. daily. Admission and tours are free. The museum is open from 9:00 A.M. to 5:00 P.M. Tuesday through Saturday (until 9:00 P.M. Friday) and 11:00 A.M. to 6:00 P.M. Sunday. Call (919) 833–1935 for more information.

WAKE FOREST

If you're looking for an opportunity for outdoor recreation, two lakes are within easy driving distance from Raleigh, as are a handful of city and county parks. In Wake Forest, north of Raleigh at the juncture of U.S. Highway 1A and State Highway 98, you'll find **Falls Lake State Recreation Area,** located on Creedmoor Road. It is one of the largest recreation facilities in the state and offers camping, hiking, fishing, swimming, a picnic area, playgrounds, boat rentals, and interpretive nature programs. Hours vary according to season. Call (919) 676–1027 for more information.

APEX

Southwest of Raleigh is **Jordan Lake Recreation Area,** located on State Park Road. Just take Highway 64 west out of Raleigh. The largest summertime home of the bald eagle in the Eastern United States, it's a great place to study nature. The 15,000-acre recreation area offers a full-service marina as well as opportunities for camping, fishing, and swimming. Hours vary according to season. Call (919) 362–0586 for more information.

SMITHFIELD

Your kids might not know exactly who Ava Gardner is, (she may be before your time, too, for that matter, but your parents will know), yet they'll probably get a kick out of a vísit to the **Ava Gardner Museum,** located on Third Street in her hometown of Smithfield, southeast of Raleigh at Interstate 95 and Highway 70. The museum was opened in 1991, a year after the actress died, as a tribute to her. Exhibits include the posters from her fifty-seven films as well as photographs that show her as a child through

Don't miss the Ava Gardner Museum, the world's largest collection of Ava Gardner memorabilia. (Courtesy the Johnson County Convention Bureau)

her years as a seductive leading lady of the 1940s and 1950s. You will find other memorabilia from her life at this unique museum, too. Admission to the museum is free. It is open from 1:00 to 5:00 P.M. daily. At this writing there were plans to move the museum to a location on Front Street. Call (919) 934–5830 for more information.

South of Smithfield on U.S. Highway 701 you'll find find **Bentonville Battleground,** the site of the state's largest battle ever fought. The fierce Civil War battle raged for three days, but Union troops eventually beat down Confederate forces, and a month later the war ended in the Carolinas. More than four thousand men were killed, wounded, or missing in the battle. Many of them were taken to the farm home of John and Amy Harper, which was turned into a field hospital. The house still stands and is furnished as a field hospital. A section of Union trenches and a cemetery remain as stark reminders of the battle. Other exhibits are on display at the site's visitor center. Admission is free. The site is open from April through October from 9:00 A.M. to 5:00 P.M. Monday through Saturday and 1:00 to 5:00 P.M. Sunday. Call (919) 594–0789 for more information.

KENLY

Life on the tobacco farm is the subject on display at the bright **Tobacco Farm Life Museum,** located on U.S. Highway 301 in Kenly, northeast of Smithfield. The exhibits at the museum show how tobacco farming improved the life of the farm families who did it. Until then farming was done only for subsistence and brought no cash. Here you can visit the Depression era of the 1930s and see artifacts that relate to the farmers' struggles. On display are school books, medical equipment, and household goods as well as tobacco farming equipment and outbuildings. Admission costs $2.00 for adults and $1.00 for children ages five through eleven. Children age four or younger get in free. Call (919) 284–3431 for more information.

BAILEY

More everyday life from the late nineteenth century is waiting at the **Country Doctor Museum,** on U.S. Highway 264 in Bailey, north of Kenley and east of Raleigh. The museum was chartered in 1967 in honor of the tradition of the family doctor. It consists of two restored offices of country doctors who practiced this way. It's easy to appreciate how the medical field has progressed when you see the artifacts here. On display are apothecary jars, old stethoscopes, and saws and knives used at battlefield hospitals. Admission is free. The museum is open from 2:00 to 5:00 P.M. Sunday through Thursday. Call (919) 235–4165 for more information.

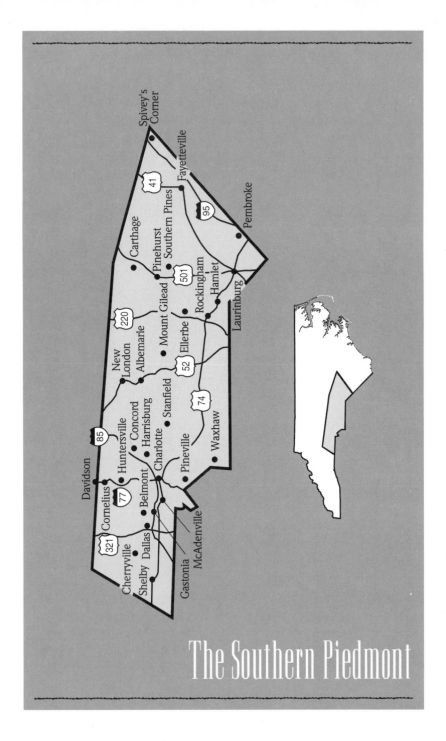

The Southern Piedmont

The Southern Piedmont

In North Carolina's Southern Piedmont your family will be treated to some of the state's biggest, best, brightest, tallest, and loudest elements. At the heart of the region is the state's biggest city, which features major-league sports, the state's largest amusement park, and what is one of the world's best science museums. Not far away, you can enjoy down-home fun at the state's largest county fair, or visit a small textile community that is set to brighten up your Christmas season. The region extends east into the Carolina heartland, where you'll find some of the country's premier golf courses and discover the unusual art of hollerin'.

Growth has made travel within some cities difficult, but getting around in this region isn't totally unpleasant. From the north, Interstate 77 bisects Charlotte and intersects with Interstate 85, which runs northeast to Greensboro and southwest into South Carolina. To get to the eastern part of the region from Greensboro, take U.S. Highway 220. From the Triangle Area take U.S. Highway 15/501. U.S. Highway 74 runs along the southern part of the region, and Interstate 95 is a good route to use when traveling the eastern part of the region.

SHELBY

Late September through early October is the time to come to Shelby, located along Highway 74 at the western end of the Southern Piedmont. It is then that thousands of people roll in for the state's largest county fair. The **Cleveland County Fair** is a traditional event featuring carnival rides, games, exhibitions, livestock shows, and contests. Plenty of homegrown food and country crafts will also be on hand for you to buy. The Cleveland County fairgrounds are located at 1751 East Marion Street (Highway 74 Business). The fair traditionally runs for ten days. Admission costs $4.75 for adults and $1.00 for children through age eleven. An additional fee is charged for many of the attractions. During the rest of the year, the fairgrounds are host to a number of festivals and horse shows. Call (704) 484–4999 for more information about Shelby.

CHERRYVILLE

In the small town of Cherryville, about a twenty-minute drive northeast of Shelby on State Highway 150, there is a small but unique museum. You can check out the old big rigs at the **C. Grier Beam Truck Museum,** 117 North Mountain Street. The museum was opened in 1982 in an old gas station that once served as the headquarters for Carolina Freight Carriers Corporation. The museum commemorates the history of trucking, and you will see trucks dating back to 1929 and displays that look back at the origin of trucking. Admission is free. The museum is open from 1:00 to 5:00 P.M. Thursday, 10:00 A.M. to 5:00 P.M. Friday, and 10:00 A.M. to 3:00 P.M. Saturday. Call (704) 435–3072 or (704) 435–1346 for more information.

DALLAS

Step back into the 1800s at one of the four-star hotels of the time at the **Gaston County Museum of Art and History,** 131 West Main Street in Dallas, a town southeast of Cherryville on State Highway 279, just east of U.S. Highway 321. Housed in the former Hoffman Hotel, built in 1852, the museum is at the center of the historic district in the former county seat. Since 1984 the museum has been working to renovate the hotel into the structure it once was. It is now occupied by displays emphasizing the county's textile heritage as well as the largest collection of horse-drawn carriages in North Carolina. You are also likely to see one of many changing art exhibits here. In addition, you can get a brochure of information on buildings included in the district's walking tour. Admission is free. The museum is open from 10:00 A.M. to 5:00 P.M. Tuesday through Friday, 1:00 to 5:00 P.M. Saturday, and 2:00 to 5:00 P.M. Sunday. Call (704) 922–7681 for more information.

GASTONIA

A good place to spend a quiet afternoon hiking or canoeing is at **Crowders Mountain State Park,** located off Highway 74 on the western end of Gastonia. The mountain's stone face, jutting 800 feet above the surrounding area, is an attraction for adventurous mountain climbers. You might even see experienced rappellers taking on the mountain's challenging terrain. You'll find several trails that are easier to climb, and you can fish in the lake or rent a canoe. The park office periodically offers interpretive nature presentations. The park generally is open during daylight hours, year-round. Admission is free. Call (704) 853–5375 for more information.

Head east on Highway 74 and right on Garrison Boulevard to the **Schiele Museum of Natural History and Planetarium.** After you have been here you won't forget it. The museum is continuing on its mission of educating Gaston County students, but it has grown to become a staple for the community. Within the museum's walls you find North Carolina Hall, showing the six regions of North Carolina during various seasons. Look on top of the cave in one three-dimensional diorama and you will see a bobcat that wags its tail every few minutes. Look carefully in the cave and you will see bats on the ceiling. The Hall of Earth and Man presents life as it developed over the last 500 million years. It's almost as if the saber-toothed tiger in one exhibit is actually alive. In addition, the museum's space theater presents shows on the arts, history, travel, and ecology, along with more traditional planetarium shows.

Outside the museum you discover more on the "Trail For All Seasons," the Eighteenth Century Backcountry Farm and the Catawba Indian Village. Interpretive and living-history programs are scheduled at the Schiele Museum throughout the year. Admission to the museum is free, but a modest admission fee may be charged for programs and shows. Hours are 9:00 A.M. to 5:00 P.M. Tuesday through Friday and 1:00 to 5:00 P.M. Saturday and Sunday. Call (704) 866–6900 for more information.

MCADENVILLE

Located between Interstate 85 and Highway 74 is McAdenville, better known as **Christmastown USA.** Each December this small textile community turns on more than 350,000 green, red, and white lights on homes, in trees, and around the small lake in the center of town. Speakers

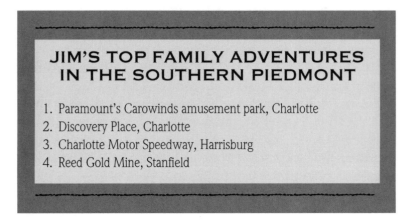

JIM'S TOP FAMILY ADVENTURES IN THE SOUTHERN PIEDMONT

1. Paramount's Carowinds amusement park, Charlotte
2. Discovery Place, Charlotte
3. Charlotte Motor Speedway, Harrisburg
4. Reed Gold Mine, Stanfield

play carols, and churches present nativity scenes in one of the state's most spectacular Christmas displays. The lights come on in early December and stay on until late in the month. The lights are on from 5:00 to 9:30 P.M. Monday through Friday and 5:00 to 11:00 P.M. Saturday and Sunday. For exact dates when the lights will be on in a particular year, call (704) 824–3190.

BELMONT

Daniel Stowe Botanical Gardens, 6500 South New Hope Road in Belmont, is accessible from Gastonia via Highway 74 or Interstate 85. Although these 450 acres of beautiful meadows and woodlands only opened as a botanical garden in 1989, it has already been featured in *Southern Living* magazine. Its beauty intensifies from one spring to the next as perennials, annuals, and daylilies burst into color. Here you will also find herb and vegetable gardens, a visitor center, and a nice gift shop. Hands-on gardening programs are presented on the weekends. The gardens are open from 9:00 A.M. to 5:00 P.M. Monday through Saturday and noon to 5:00 P.M. Sunday. For more information call (704) 825–4490.

CHARLOTTE

The Queen City is North Carolina's largest city and is the center for arts, culture, and big-league sports. With a population of nearly a half a million,

Charlotte became a national financial center in the late 1980s and early 1990s as local resident NationsBank grew to become one of the largest banks in America. This growth only strengthened the financial stability created through Charlotte/Douglas International Airport, which opened the city to the world and made it a transportation hub for the Southeast. But this growth has meant more than additions to the uptown (not downtown) skyline. The city has seen a proverbial boom in the creation of more fun things to see and do. For information on accommodations or for general information on the city, call the Charlotte Visitor's Information Center at (704) 331-2700.

The most notable of the city's changes came in November 1988, when the NBA's Charlotte Hornets descended on the **Charlotte Coliseum** and transformed it into "The Hive." The 24,000-seat coliseum, located just off the Billy Graham Parkway, is more than a home to the basketball team. It hosts dozens of events year-round, including college basketball games, Charlotte Rage arena football games, concerts, and special events, such as "Disney on Ice." Perhaps the best time to see the coliseum is in the fall, when the Hornets host Fan Appreciation Day during the preseason. The free event includes a short practice, an opportunity to get autographs, tours of the facility, and carnival rides and games. The Hornets have set NBA attendance records since their first season, so you'll have to plan ahead or be creative to get tickets to a game. Single-game tickets go on sale after the NBA schedule is released in late summer. You can call the Hornets office at (704) 357-0252 for more information or call the coliseum at (704) 357-4700.

Charlotte's most recent addition to its sports entourage came in 1993, when it was awarded an NFL expansion team. Almost immediately the city began construction of the 72,000-seat **Carolina Panthers Stadium.** The stadium, located uptown, was still under construction during the Panthers' inaugural season in 1995, so they played that season at Clemson University's Death Valley in South Carolina. Tickets for single games, on sale in early May, go quickly. Call (704) 358-1644 for more information.

Charlotte's third major sports venue is **Independence Arena,** the home of the Charlotte Checkers, a minor-league hockey team. The 10,000-seat arena, located on Independence Boulevard, once served as Charlotte's primary center for sporting and entertainment, but now it mainly functions as the Checkers' home and as host to other smaller attractions. When the Checkers aren't playing hockey, the ice is open on an irregular basis for public skating. Call (704) 335–3100 for more information.

If you're finished spectating, get ready for some active fun. Just 10 miles south of Charlotte on Interstate 77, at the North Carolina–South Carolina border, is **Paramount's Carowinds** amusement park. The state's largest theme park is packed with a day full of fun and adventure for everyone in the family. As you walk through the main gate, you'll be greeted by your favorite characters from *Star Trek: The Next Generation.* Younger children will adore the characters in Hanna Barbera Land, where you won't want to miss the Scooby-Doo roller coaster—a thrill for everyone from about age five to fifty. A county fair section includes games and rides for all ages. Included are bumper cars, a NASCAR simulation, and more.

There's plenty at Carowinds for older children, teens, and Mom and

You don't have to look far to find adventure at Paramount's Carowinds amusement park. (Courtesy Paramount's Carowinds)

Dad, too. Check out North America's first movie-themed wooden roller coaster—dubbed "The Hurler"—in Wayne's World. This is an interesting section of the park because you'll feel like you're actually walking behind the scenes of a Hollywood set. The truly adventurous will want to experience the "Vortex," a standup roller coaster and the "Drop Zone," which drops visitors 174 feet at more than 50 miles per hour. You can cool off at the Rip Tide Reef water section. For a break in the action, you'll want to catch some of the shows at the park, including the spectacular *Paramount on Ice,* which salutes Paramount Communications movie and television productions.

Free kennels are provided if your pet is with you, and picnic facilities are available if you aren't lured into one of the park's dozens of food stands and restaurants. Admission to the park changes from season to season, but plan to spend more than $20 per adult and more than $10 for children ages four, five, and six. Children age three or younger get in free. The park is open from 10:00 A.M. to 8:00 P.M. Saturday and Sunday only in March, April, May, September, and through mid-October. It's open from 10:00 A.M. to 8:00 P.M. daily from June through mid-August. Call (800) 888–4386 for more information.

Whatever has drawn you to Charlotte, you won't want to miss a chance to see **Discovery Place,** a national-award-winning, hands-on science and technology center. The complex also includes a state-of-the-art planetarium and the *Charlotte Observer* OMNIMAX Theater. Located at 301 North Tryon, you can enter a three-story rainforest, explore outer space, or learn about the intricacies of the human body. Best of all, the kids can touch all they want. Some of the most interesting exhibits include the Challenger Learning Center, which features mission control and a space station; an aquarium and tidal pool; the Life Center; and the Science Circus, where you can perform experiments yourself.

The OMNIMAX, considered to be the best motion picture system in the world, is comprised of the largest screen in history and a six-track sound system. The Space Voyager Planetarium features a space ball that projects 10,000 stars onto the country's largest dome and 200 special effects projectors. Presentations at the OMNIMAX and planetarium are scheduled throughout the year.

Kids can really get involved at Discovery Place, a great science and technology center. (Courtesy Discovery Place)

Admission to the museum exhibit halls starts at $5.50 for adults, $4.50 for children ages six through twelve, and $2.75 for children ages three through five. Combination tickets, which also get you into the theater or planetarium, start at $7.50 for adults, $6.50 for children ages six through twelve, and $5.50 for children ages three to five. Discovery Place hours are 9:00 A.M. to 5:00 P.M. Monday through Friday, 9:00 A.M. to 6:00 P.M. Saturday, and 1:00 to 6:00 P.M. Sunday. OMNIMAX shows are held during operating hours, except on Sunday, and at 7:00 P.M. Thursday through Saturday. Planetarium shows are at 9:30 A.M. and 2:00 P.M. Monday through Wednesday, at 9:30 A.M. and 2:00 and 6:00 P.M. Thursday through Saturday, and at 2:00 and 6:00 P.M. Sunday. Discovery Place is closed Thanksgiving and Christmas days. Call (704) 372–6261 for more information.

You can plan to spend several hours in this part of downtown. A variety of shops and restaurants abound. Just around the corner from Discovery Place, you can wander into **Spirit Square,** located at 345 North

College Street. This arts center features artisans working on their crafts for people to watch. It also serves as a venue for the Charlotte Symphony (704–332–0468) and the Charlotte Repertory Theater (704–333–8587). The center features all varieties of art, including seven galleries and three theaters. Call Spirit Square at (704) 376–8883.

For one weekend each April, uptown Charlotte is converted into a classic street fair for **SpringFest,** which has become the city's largest annual celebration. The event not only welcomes the coming of spring, but celebrates the arts as well. It attracts hundreds of thousands of people each year to take in the visual, performance, and culinary arts. Here you can dance to your choice of music as live bands play on five stages throughout the festival. In addition, a kids' spot lets youngsters try their hands at a variety of art projects. Call (704) 372–7469 for more information.

Shopping and dining are available in **Founders Hall,** part of Nations-Bank Corporate Center, the tallest building in the Southeast. The glass-enclosed center, located at 100 North Tryon Street, is dominated by a 10,000-square-foot winter garden and fountain. Here you can browse or dine in a number of upscale shops and restaurants. In addition, the hall serves as the location for various community functions and celebrations throughout the year. Among these events is **First Night,** the city's all-out New Year's Eve celebration. It's an alcohol-free event that features entertainment and art activities presented throughout downtown. First Night (704–372–9667) costs $10 per person except children two or younger, who get in free. Founders Hall is open from 10:00 A.M. to 6:00 P.M. Monday through Friday and 10:00 A.M. to 4:00 P.M. Saturday. Call (704) 386–0117 for more information.

For culture, a visit to the **Mint Museum of Art,** 2730 Randolph Road, is a must. To get there, take Trade Street east, then turn right on Queens Road and left on Randolph Road. Built in 1836 as the first branch of the U.S. Mint, it later served as a Confederate headquarters, a hospital, and an assay office. In 1933, it was moved from its original location uptown and opened as North Carolina's first museum of art three years later. Here you'll see a complete set of gold coins minted there, American and European paintings, pre-Columbian art, historic costumes, and ancient Chinese ceramics. You'll also see life-size paintings of King George III and his queen, Charlotte, for whom the city was named. Seeing the queen's carriage will round out your trip to the museum. Admission costs $4.00 for anyone age twelve or older and is free for children age eleven or younger. Everyone gets in free from 5:00 to 10:00 P.M. Tuesday and the second Sunday of each month. In addition to Tuesday's evening hours, the museum is open from 10:00 A.M. to 5:00 P.M. Tuesday through Saturday and 1:00 to 6:00 P.M. Sunday. The museum is closed Christmas and New Year's Day. Call (704) 337–2000 for more information.

A really first-class place to take the kids for exposure to art is the **Children's Theatre of Charlotte,** 1017 East Morehead Street. The theater is largely dedicated to use of the arts in education and is heavily involved with the Mecklenburg County school system. Many of the plays are performed by local children; however, its playbill includes several professionally produced productions annually. In the past the theater has presented such gems as *Winnie the Pooh, Treasure Island,* and *Charlotte's Web*, in addition to creative holiday and seasonal productions. Tickets start at $6.00. Call (704) 333–8983 for more information.

Next, head to the **Nature Museum.** At 1658 Sterling Road, this museum is geared to younger children. It has a number of hands-on exhibits, such as games and push-button displays, to help explain natural history. It also features a puppet theater; a live animal room that includes owls, snakes and other nocturnal creatures; and a nature trail. You'll also want to see the talking Grandpa Tree, a mechanical replica of a tree that helps explain some of nature's wonders during special programs that are held nearly every weekend. Admission is $2.00 for anyone over the age of three and is free for children under three. Hours are 9:00 A.M. to 5:00 P.M. Monday through Friday, 10:00 A.M. to 5:00 P.M. Saturday, and 1:00 to 5:00 P.M. Sunday. It's closed on Thanksgiving and Christmas. For information, call (704) 332–5018.

Before or after you visit the nature museum, you can get away from the hustle and bustle of Charlotte traffic at adjacent **Freedom Park,** one of Charlotte's oldest parks and a longtime favorite for school field trips. Take along a picnic lunch. The kids will be thrilled to climb on the military equipment on the park's playground. The park is the site of **Festival in the Park,** another of Charlotte's big annual celebrations. The six-day event, held in late September, is a huge arts, crafts, and entertainment event. For more information call (704) 331–2700.

Like most towns in the Old North State, Charlotte isn't without a rich historical heritage. To get a glimpse of this history, a good place to start is at the **Charlotte Museum of History & Hezekiah Alexander Homesite,** located at 3500 Shamrock Drive. Built in 1774, the home is the oldest dwelling in Mecklenburg County. The house includes a museum with exhibits that concentrate on the history of the city. In the two-story springhouse you'll see a hand-hewn log kitchen with a working rock fireplace. Admission to the museum and gardens is free, but admission to the house costs $2.00 for adults and $1.00 for young people ages six to sixteen. Children age five or younger get in free. The site is open from 10:00 A.M. to 5:00 P.M. Tuesday through Friday and 2:00 to 5:00 P.M. Saturday and Sunday. Guided tours are presented at 1:15 and 3:15 P.M. Tuesday through Friday and at 2:15 and 3:15 P.M. Saturday and Sunday. Call (704) 568–1774 for more information.

HUNTERSVILLE

While you're in the Charlotte area, plan to spend some time exploring the towns along Interstate 77, north of the city, as well as at **Lake Norman,** the largest artificial lake in North Carolina. It's a big draw for boating and fishing enthusiasts from across the state. Built by Duke Power Company to accommodate its hydroelectric and nuclear power plants, you'll find ten public access areas around the 32,500-acre lake for camping, swimming, and fishing. Duke Power has also established a 1,400-acre public park north of Huntersville.

Huntersville is the home of the **Loch Norman Highland Games,** a three-day festival that celebrates the pageantry of the Scottish heritage of the region. Held in late April off Old Statesville Road, the games feature traditional Scottish competitions, such as the caber toss, a 56-pound weight throw, dancing, and sheepdog herding. You can also enjoy authentic music from bagpipes, Celtic harps, and fiddles. Of course, plenty of food is on hand as well. Call (704) 875–3113 for more information.

A good place to visit in Huntersville is **Latta Plantation Park,** 5225 Sample Road. The 760-acre park borders Mountain Island Lake and includes an interpretive center, equestrian center, and hiking and horse trails. Also at the park is the **Carolina Raptor Center,** which provides care for injured or sick birds of prey. Educational exhibits and programs are presented at the center, and you can take a walk along the nature trail, where hawks, owls, and bald eagles are on display. In addition, the park presents living-history tours of the James Latta house on the first and third Thursdays of each month. The two-story Federal-style house, built in 1800, is elaborately decorated to match the intricate detail of the architecture.

The park is open during daylight hours, and facilities are free. Call (704) 875–1391 for more information. Admission to the raptor center costs $2.00 for adults and $1.00 for children up to age eleven. Hours are 10:00 A.M. to 5:00 P.M. Tuesday through Sunday. Call (704) 875–6521 for more information. Admission to the Latta home costs $2.00 for adults and $1.00 for children. The house is open from 9:00 A.M. to 5:00 P.M. Tuesday through Saturday and 1:00 to 5:00 P.M. Sunday. Call (704) 875–2312 for more information.

CORNELIUS

In Cornelius you'll find **Duke Power's Energy Explorium,** located on the lake off State Highway 73. The explorium presents hands-on exhibits where you can throw the switches on model nuclear and coal-fired plants. You can power a television by converting your body's energy on a treadmill, play computer games, and figure out how much energy you get for a dollar. Admission is free. The explorium is open year-round, from 9:00 A.M. to 5:00 P.M. Monday through Saturday. Sunday hours are noon to 6:00 P.M. from June through August and noon to 5:00 P.M. from September through May.

DAVIDSON

The **Carolina Renaissance Festival** in Davidson, just north of Cornelius, is quickly becoming one of the area's biggest attractions. Each fall, sixteenth-century Europe is recreated during weekends in October and November. Don't be surprised to find youself at the edge of a jousting contest or in the middle of a sword fight. You can enjoy the antics of the court jester and see knights dressed in full armor. Finding a feast fit for a king, complete with big turkey legs, won't be any problem, either. And when you finish eating, you can browse through acres of shops and galleries. Advance tickets cost $9.95 for adults, $3.95 for children ages five through eleven, and children under five get in free. Call (704) 896–5544 for more information.

PINEVILLE

Now let's head south of Charlotte to Pineville, the birthplace and child-hood home of the eleventh president of the United States. The **James K. Polk Memorial,** located on U.S. Highway 521, features exhibits on his life and times. You can see an audiovisual display here as well as take a guided tour of the home. Admission is free. From April through October, the site is open from 9:00 A.M. to 5:00 P.M. Monday through Saturday and 1:00 to 5:00 P.M. Sunday. The rest of the year it's open from 10:00 A.M. to 4:00 P.M. Tuesday through Saturday and 1:00 to 5:00 P.M. Sunday. Call (704) 889–7145 for more information.

To give the kids a treat for lunch or dinner, **Celebration Station,** 10400 Cadillac Street, is always a big hit. The amusement center/restau-rant offers delicious pizza and a chance to let the kids run off some steam. Every one in the family might want to ride go-carts or bumper boats, or even play a round of miniature golf. Younger children can play in Harry's Clubhouse, a play park with rides designed especially for them, and older kids can brush up on their batting at the cages. The cost to enter Harry's Clubhouse is $7.99. Miniature golf, bumper boats, go carts, and rides for children and adults over 56 inches tall cost $3.50. A combination ticket that allows you to ride as much as you want costs $13.99. Hours vary, but generally Celebration Station is open from 4:00 to 9:00 P.M. Monday through Thursday, 4:00 to 11:00 P.M. Friday, noon to 11:00 P.M. Saturday, and noon to 9:00 P.M. Sunday. Call (704) 552–7888 for more information.

WAXHAW

Traveling south on Highway 16 from Charlotte will take you to Waxhaw, an area rich in Native American history. That history is presented each June in *Listen and Remember.* The musical drama, which was locally written, is a production of the Waxhaw Historical Festival and Drama

Association. It has been revised over its thirty-plus years in production. The outdoor performance leads you though history, beginning with settlers moving in on local Native American territories, to the Revolutionary War, to the life of Andrew Jackson, the seventh president of the United States, who was born near here. The play is performed each Friday and Saturday in June at the Waxhaw Amphitheater. Tickets are $6.00 for adults and $2.50 for children under twelve. Call (704) 843–2300 for ticket information.

Where in the world did words come from? That question is answered at the **Museum of the Alphabet,** an unusual but enticing collection of exhibits that traces the early origins of written communication from ancient times through the development of the Roman alphabet to our English alphabet today. You can also see a working model of the first printing press, displays on alphabets of foreign languages, and descriptions of the systems of alphabets created for the deaf and blind. Admission is free, but donations are accepted. The museum is open from 9:00 A.M. to noon and 1:00 to 3:30 P.M. Monday through Saturday. Call (704) 843–6066 for more information.

To enjoy outdoor recreation for a day, or even a weekend, try **Cane Creek Park,** 5213 Harkey Road. The park offers you an opportunity to wet a line at the trophy bass lake, rent a paddleboat, or take a swim in cool, clear water. Cane Creek also offers three campsites to accommodate tents or recreational vehicles with prices ranging from $10 to $29 per night. Also, you can enjoy miles of scenic hiking trails or splashing around in a canoe ($20 per day) or row boat ($15 per day). The park also offers sports equipment rental and a chance to play miniature golf. A separate fee is charged for each of the amenities the park has to offer, but the most expensive is $2.50. An entrance fee of $2.00 per car is also charged. The park generally is open during daylight hours, daily during the summer and only on weekends the rest of the year. Call (704) 843–3919 for more information.

HARRISBURG

This is a high-speed zone—the home of the **Charlotte Motor Speedway**—accessible from Interstate 85 from Charlotte or U.S. Highway 601 from

Monroe. Thousands of NASCAR fans from across the country flock here each May and October to watch their favorite drivers negotiate speeds up to nearly 200 miles per hour at one of the country's premier racing facilities. The **Coca-Cola 600,** held each Memorial Day weekend, draws a huge crowd—second only in size to the Indianapolis 500, which is held the same day. As crowds roll in by recreational vehicle, truck, and car, the entire area lights up with races and activities all month long. Excitement also picks up in October with races culminating with the running of the **UAW-GM Quality 500.** Call (704) 455–3200 for ticket information.

In addition to these major sporting events, the Charlotte Motor Speedway hosts the **Legends Car Summer Shootout** each Tuesday during the summer. Legends cars are small replicas of 1937 and 1940 Fords and Chevrolets. Games, other spectator events, activities, and entertainment from the world's fastest mascot, Lug Nut, are on hand. Tickets, available only at the gate, cost $5.00 for adults and $1.00 for children ages seven through eleven. Pit passes are available for $12.00 per person.

Other events held at the speedway include auto shows, motorcycle racing, go-cart racing, and tours of this spectacular facility. On these tours, you visit the garages, pits, and winner's circle. When the track is not in use, you can take a trip around the track. Finally, pick out a gift for a Winston Cup fan you know at the gift shop. Tour admission costs $4.00 per person, with children age two or younger admitted free. Tours are held from 9:00 A.M. to 5:00 P.M. Monday through Saturday and noon to 5:00 P.M. Sunday, except when racing events are scheduled. Call (704) 455–3204 for more information on tours.

Next to the speedway, you can visit **Memory Lane Museum and Gift Shop.** Step back into the 1950s at this unique museum that presents classic cars and dragsters from years gone by. You will also see memorabilia and cars from the sport of racing. The gift shop features a huge selection of unique 1950s and race-related souvenirs and gifts. Admission costs $4.00 for adults and $3.00 for children ages seven through seventeen, or the whole family can get in for $8.00. The facility is usually open seven days a week, but hours may vary according to activity at the speedway. Call (704) 788–9494 for more information.

CONCORD

Fancy Feathers Farm Zoo, located northeast of Harrisburg off Highway 49 at 1643 Simplicity Road, offers twenty-five acres of down-home fun. Here you can see dozens of exotic animals, including zebras, monkeys, bison, and camels. You can either hike the trail along peaceful streams or take a golf cart. Admission price is $5.00 for adults and $3.00 for children. Hours are 9:00 A.M. to 9:00 P.M. Monday through Saturday and noon to 7:00 P.M. Sunday. Call (704) 782–3149 for more information.

STANFIELD

Some say there could still be gold in Stanfield. You can try to come up with some of it as you pan for gold at **Reed Gold Mine,** 9621 Reed Mine Road off State Highway 200. From Concord, take Highway 601, then turn south on Highway 200. Here you will experience the country's first gold rush, which started with the discovery of a nugget (big enough to be used as a doorstop) near here in 1799. North Carolina remained the leader of gold production until the California Gold Rush in 1848. Today, visitors at the site can see a film on more of this history, exhibits on the mining process, and the tools the miners used. In addition, you can see the underground tunnels of the nation's first gold mine. Admission is free. From April through October, the site is open from 9:00 A.M. to 5:00 P.M. Monday through Saturday and 1:00 to 5:00 P.M. Sunday. From November through March, the site is open from 10:00 A.M. to 4:00 P.M. Tuesday through Saturday and 1:00 to 4:00 P.M. Sunday. The panning area is open on a seasonal basis.

ALBEMARLE

From the Reed Gold Mine, Highway 24/27 will take you to the pretty historic town of Albemarle, near the border of the Uwharrie National Forest. While this isn't a famous tourist area, it offers a handful of attractions, mainly ample opportunity to enjoy the outdoors. But first take a trip to the historic downtown area, which served as a cultural and commercial haven for the rural area in the late 1800s and early 1900s. The Stanley County Chamber of Commerce (704–982–8116) can provide you with a walking map of the downtown area, where you'll see many charms from the late

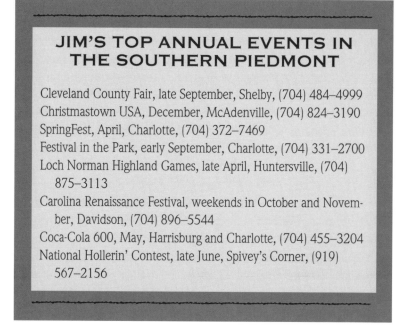

JIM'S TOP ANNUAL EVENTS IN THE SOUTHERN PIEDMONT

Cleveland County Fair, late September, Shelby, (704) 484–4999
Christmastown USA, December, McAdenville, (704) 824–3190
SpringFest, April, Charlotte, (704) 372–7469
Festival in the Park, early September, Charlotte, (704) 331–2700
Loch Norman Highland Games, late April, Huntersville, (704) 875–3113
Carolina Renaissance Festival, weekends in October and November, Davidson, (704) 896–5544
Coca-Cola 600, May, Harrisburg and Charlotte, (704) 455–3204
National Hollerin' Contest, late June, Spivey's Corner, (919) 567–2156

nineteenth and early twentieth centuries. You can get a glimpse of the art deco style of architecture of the 1920s at the **Albemarle Opera House** or at the **Alameda Theater,** where silent films once played. Both are located near East Main Street.

North of downtown you'll find **Morrow Mountain State Park,** which offers the beautiful crystal-clear waters of the adjacent Lake Tillery. The landscape of this mountain area, located in the heart of the foothills, is interesting. Because they were formed by volcanic eruptions thousands of years ago, the hills have resisted erosion and maintained a rugged appearance against a beautiful backdrop of green in the spring and summer. You'll find a number of trails in the park, ranging in length from a half mile to 6 miles. A small natural history museum, located at the center of the park, explains the development of the region and includes exhibits on the wildlife and the vegetation that occupy the area. Admission is free to the park and nature center. A family camping area can accommodate tents and recreational vehicles year-round, but there are no facility hookups. Water, showers, and toilets are available nearby. If you want to stay for a week, you can rent one of six cabins in the park, from April through October. In addition to the rich nature, the park also has a swimming pool and boat and canoe rentals. Admission to the park is free, but camping sites cost $5.00 per night, boats and canoes rent for $2.50 per hour, and pool fees are $2.00 for adults and $1.00 for children through eleven years of age. The park opens at 8:00 A.M. and generally closes at dusk. Call (704) 982–4402 for more information.

NEW LONDON

More camping facilities and a shot at striking it rich are available north of Albemarle at the **Cotton Patch Gold Mine,** located just off U.S. Highway 52 at State Highway 740. The campground accommodates tent camping as well as full facility hookups for recreational vehicles, in addition to rest rooms and showers. You can pan for gold and other minerals here. For a single fee of $7.00 you get equipment and instructions on how to pan. From March through October, the mine is open from 9:00 A.M. to 5:00 P.M. daily. Call (704) 463–5797 for more information.

MOUNT GILEAD

If you head southeast of Albemarle on State Highway 73 through Mount Gilead, you'll find the **Town Creek Indian Mound,** a ceremonial center for the Creek Indian Nation that occupied the area as early as 1450. The site, which served as a meeting place for the clans, religious ceremonies, and even executions of enemies 300 years ago, has been rebuilt nearly to completion over the past 50 years. The earthen mound—a sort of stage— is encircled by a wall constructed of logs, bound together by cane, and several other structures made of dirt, sticks, and thatch. Presentations are held to explain the structure, the history of the Indians, and the research that has been done in the area. Admission to the site is free. From April through October hours are 9:00 A.M. to 5:00 P.M. Monday through Saturday and 1:00 to 5:00 P.M. Sunday. From November through March hours are 10:00 A.M. to 4:00 P.M. Tuesday through Saturday and 1:00 to 4:00 P.M. Sunday. Call (919) 439–6802 for more information.

ELLERBE

Runners from all over the Southeast come to the small town of Ellerbe (from Mount Gilead, head southeast on Highway 73 and turn south on Highway 220) each April for one of the state's most demanding marathons. The 26-mile course is extremely hilly and demanding and has enjoyed increasing success over the past several years. In addition, the **Rankin Museum of American Heritage,** located on West Church Street, is a heralded collection that offers you an opportunity to travel back in time all over the world. The museum is a diverse collection of exhibits and artifacts used to explain the heritage of North America, South America, Central America, and Africa. Here you'll see displays such as a fierce polar bear, a Central American jaguar, and a host of moose, elk, and caribou. In addition, the museum features displays on Indian life and a fine mineral collection. Admission costs $2.00 for adults and $1.00 for children through age seventeen. Museum hours are 10:00 A.M. to 4:00 P.M. Tuesday through Friday and 2:00 to 5:00 P.M. Saturday and Sunday. Call (919) 652–6378 for more information.

ROCKINGHAM

Highway 220 South is the route to Rockingham, another hub for NASCAR racing and more high-speed action. The **North Carolina Motor Speedway** and the **Rockingham Dragway,** located on Highway 1, which also runs through Rockingham, are host to two major Winston Cup races and two Grand National races each year. In addition, the racetracks hold sports car, motorcycle, and go-cart races as well as auto shows and other events throughout the year. Call the speedway at (910) 582–2861 or the dragway at (910) 582–3400 for more information.

HAMLET

Highway 74 will take you southeast out of Rockingham to Hamlet. A hall of fame for railroads exists here at the **National Railroad Museum,** 2 Main Street. The museum is located in the old Seaboard Air Line Railway depot, built in 1900. The kids will love the extravagant Model Train Layout that features the Orange Blossom Special and the Silver Meteor. The exhibit is designed as the system was in the early twentieth century. The museum also includes artifacts, photographs, and maps preserving the railway's heritage, which was once crucial to the area. Admission is free, but the museum is supported totally by donations. The museum and railroad hall of fame are open from 10:00 A.M. to 5:00 P.M. Saturday and 1:00 to 5:00 P.M. Sunday.

PINEHURST

From Hamlet, take Highway 177 north to Highway 1. Known as the "Golf Capital of the World," **Pinehurst** and the surrounding area offer the best amenities for those who play golf and much more. In addition to world-class golf competition, the area also supports tennis competitions and equestrian events throughout the year. International cycling teams have also begun training here. You'll find more than thirty-five championship golf courses that fill the area, not to mention the dozens of plush resorts. Pinehurst Number Two is scheduled as the site for the 1999 U.S. Open Championship.

The **PGA World Golf Hall of Fame** is located at the junction of Highway 15/501 and State Highway 211 in Pinehurst. The displays here take you back 500 years to the invention of the game in Scotland. Exhibits and photographs highlight some of the greatest moments in the game of golf. You'll also see how balls and clubs are designed and made. Admission costs $3.00 for adults and $2.00 for young people ages ten through seventeen. The hall of fame is open from March through November from 9:00 A.M. to 5:00 P.M. daily. Call (919) 295–6651 for more information.

SOUTHERN PINES

To get from Pinehurst to Southern Pines, take Highway 5. The **Weymouth Woods Nature Preserve,** 400 North Fort Bragg Road, south of Southern Pines, offers an introspective look at the natural features of the area. Here you will find 750 acres of wildflowers, wildlife, and peaceful rolling streams. The preserve includes more than 4 miles of hiking trails, a beaver pond, and a nature museum. At the museum, you can see how the area evolved and hear a night sounds display that highlights the nocturnal wildlife of the Sandhills region. Each Sunday in the spring and summer, a nature study program is presented by a naturalist. Admission is free. The preserve is open from 9:00 A.M. to 6:00 P.M. Monday through Saturday (until 7:00 P.M. during daylight savings time) and noon to 5:00 P.M. Sunday. Call (919) 692–2167 for more information.

CARTHAGE

North of Pinehurst and Southern Pines, you'll find Carthage at the intersection of Highways 22 and 24/27. You'll want to see the **House in the Horseshoe,** 324 Alston House Road, about 10 miles north of Carthage in a bend in the Deep River. Built in 1772, this cotton plantation home features a gabled roof and big Flemish Bond chimneys. Bullet holes in some of the house's walls are evidence of the Revolutionary War battles fought on the grounds. One of those battles is re-created each August. Admission to the home is free, but hours vary. Call (919) 947–2051 for more information.

LAURINBURG

The town of Laurinburg has a rich Native American heritage. To get here, simply travel south on Highway 15/501 from the Southern Pines area or east on Highway 74 from Hamlet and visit the **Indian Museum of the Carolinas,** located on Turnpike Road. It features dozens of exhibits on Carolina Indian life, including many examples of art and some archeological artifacts. Admission is free. The museum is open from 10:00 A.M. to noon and 1:00 to 4:00 P.M. Wednesday and Thursday and 1:00 to 4:00 P.M. Sunday. Call (910) 276–5880 for more information.

PEMBROKE

Robeson County, located to the south of the Southern Pines area, is home to 26,000 Lumbee Indians, who were recognized neither by the Cherokee Nation nor as U.S. citizens before the Civil War. The town of Pembroke, located east of Laurinburg and just north off of Highway 74, relives the Lumbee struggle to overcome this oppression each summer during *Strike at the Wind,* a wonderful outdoor drama. The play depicts the life of the leader of the Lumbee, Henry Berry Lowrie, and his people in their struggles during the Civil War. Lowrie was crucial in the Lumbee efforts to free themselves from slavery and eventually win voting rights. The play is presented from early July to early September each year at the Lakeside

Amphitheater, located off State Highway 711. Tickets cost $7.00 for adults and $4.00 for children ages four through eleven. Call (910) 521–3112 for more information.

FAYETTEVILLE

More than 200 years of history are presented in Fayetteville, the location of one of the largest military bases in the world—**Fort Bragg.** With a population of 130,000 active military personnel and their families, the sprawling base is open to the public. (Nearby Pope Air Force Base is not open to the public.) You can tour the 200 square miles of the military reservation to see both contemporary military life and the U.S. history of war. You can call the base for general information at (910) 396–5401 or visit the information center on Randolph Street, which is open from 8:30 A.M. to 4:30 P.M. Monday through Friday and 9:00 A.M. to 4:00 P.M. Saturday and Sunday. Daily parachute drops are an exciting attraction for visitors to see. Call (910) 396–6366 for information on drop schedules.

The first thing you'll want to see at Fort Bragg is the **82nd Airborne Division Museum,** featuring thousands of artifacts from this internationally famous division. Items on display include helmets, weapons, parachutes, and more from World War I to Operation Desert Storm. A film on the division's history is also presented. Admission is free. The museum is open from 10:00 A.M. to 4:30 P.M. Tuesday through Saturday and 11:30 A.M. to 4:00 P.M. Sunday. Call (910) 432–3443 for more information.

The **John F. Kennedy Special Warfare Museum** at Fort Bragg features exhibits on unconventional forms of warfare, including displays on the Green Berets and Special Operation Units. You'll also see military art and cultural items from around the world. Admission is free. The museum is open from 11:30 A.M. to 4:00 P.M. Tuesday through Sunday. Call (910) 432–4272 for more information.

While touring the base you'll come across a number of memorials to those who gave their lives in various wars. At the **JFK Chapel** you'll see stained-glass windows memorializing the Green Berets plus a monument that the late actor John Wayne designed and donated to the base. Some of the tombstones at the **Fort Bragg Cemetery** date back to 1918.

More attractions are waiting for you in Fayetteville, many of them historical. You can get a brochure for a self-guided tour of the city's historical homes and buildings at the Fayetteville Convention and Visitors Bureau, 515 Ramsey Street, or call (800) 255–8217 for more information. Among the sites you'll see are the **First Presbyterian Church,** at the corner of Bow and Ann streets. Built in 1816, it is a brilliant example of Southern Colonial architecture and features a wooden truss roof. Inside you'll see lovely whale oil chandeliers, communion silver, and handmade wrought iron locks. Admission is free. Visiting hours are 8:00 A.M. to 4:30 P.M. Monday through Friday. Sunday services are held at 8:30 and 10:55 A.M. Call (910) 483–0121 for more information.

You can get an overall look at the history of the area at the **Museum of the Cape Fear,** 801 Arsenal Avenue. Exhibits here include some very old Native American artifacts, such as clothes, tools, and even children's toys. Some of the items are prehistoric in age. Admission is free. The museum is open 10:00 A.M. to 5:00 P.M. Tuesday through Saturday and 1:00 to 5:00 P.M. Sunday. Call (910) 432–5307 for more information.

SPIVEY'S CORNER

From Fayetteville, take Interstate 95 north to Highway 13 east to arrive at the home of the **National Hollerin' Contest.** That's right! The best wind pipes in the country show up here for the annual event held the third Saturday of June. Since 1969 the contest has featured the lost art of hog callin'— also an early way of communicating for folks living on neighboring farms. Now the event gets national attention, with winners regularly appearing on *The Late Show With David Letterman* and other talk shows. In addition to being entertained by the champion hollerers, you'll find crafts, gospel and country music, and plenty of food. Other contests include whistlin', conch shell and fox horn blowin', junior hollerin', and ladies callin'. Admission is $3.00, but pre-school children get in free. The event runs from 11:00 A.M. to 7:00 P.M. For more information call (919) 567–2156.

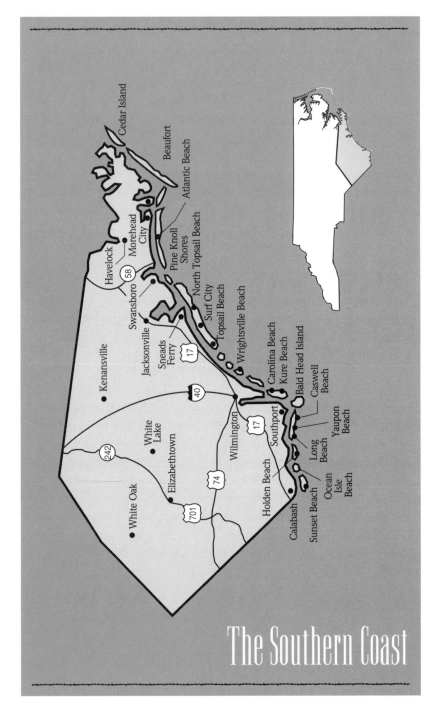

Cedar Island

Beaufort

Atlantic Beach

Havelock

Morehead City

Pine Knoll Shores

North Topsail Beach

58

Swansboro

Surf City

Topsail Beach

Jacksonville

Sneads Ferry

Wrightsville Beach

17

Kenansville

Carolina Beach

Kure Beach

Bald Head Island

Caswell Beach

40

Yaupon Beach

White Lake

Wilmington

17

Southport

Long Beach

242

Elizabethtown

74

Holden Beach

Ocean Isle Beach

White Oak

701

Calabash

Sunset Beach

The Southern Coast

The Southern Coast

Grab a blanket and the sunscreen. Plan to relax, play in the surf and sand, enjoy fresh seafood, or take a boat ride. North Carolina's Southern Coast is full of southern-facing beaches that make for calm waters and warm winds. This region is comprised of the Coastal Plain, the southern tip of the Outer Banks, Cape Lookout National Seashore, and the South Brunswick Islands —a series of small barrier islands.

While many of these islands, and the communities on them, don't offer an immense number of tourist attractions, you're likely to find that it's a great place to set up housekeeping at a cottage for a week and take any number of day trips. In addition, you will find some of the best golf courses in the Carolinas, a unique community that features seafood restaurants and two of the state's educational aquariums. Here you can also learn a lot about history from the eighteenth century to World War II.

Your adventure on the Southern Coast begins in the **Bladen Lakes** area, where you'll find a beach long before you get to the coast. The best route to take from the Charlotte area is U.S. Highway 74. From Raleigh, Interstate 40 is a speedy route right into Wilmington. U.S. Highway 17 runs the length of the coast, but it goes through many towns, so travel is generally slow. Use it to move from town to town and stick to the major highways for longer travel.

WHITE OAK

As you head into this area, the first stop you will want to make is at **Harmony Hall,** located on Route 1, just off State Highway 53 in White Oak.

Built in 1760, Harmony Hall is one of the oldest plantations in North Carolina and was once home to the state's first constitutionally elected governor, Richard Caswell. During the Revolutionary War, British General
Charles Cornwallis commandeered the home. Today it is open Sunday
afternoons with live demonstrations of broom making, soap making and
blacksmithing from 2:00 until 4:00 P.M. Admission is free, but donations
are accepted. A period re-enactment is held and wagon rides are offered
during the annual **Harmony Hall Reunion Picnic** the first Saturday in
May. For more information call (910) 866–4574.

ELIZABETHTOWN

Turnbull Creek State Forest, located north of Elizabethtown on State
Highway 242, was founded in 1986 and is still under development. Visitors to the park can take one of several trails, including the fire control trail,
where you can explore the park's fire-fighting equipment and scout plane.
The forest caters mainly to schools in the area, but some of the educational
programs may be available from the rangers at the forest office. Picnic facilities are available as well. **Jones Lake State Park,** located in the forest,
offers recreational activities within its 2,200 acres. Here you can camp,
fish, hike, and swim. The forest is open from March 15 to November 15,
from 8:30 A.M. to 4:30 P.M. Monday through Friday. Admission is free. For
more information call (910) 588–4161. The park is generally open during
daylight hours. You can reach the Jones Lake office at (910) 588–4550.

Another good place for a picnic is the historic **Troy Hole Battleground.** The battleground is located in a ravine that runs from downtown
Elizabethtown to the Cape Fear River. The park includes a playground, picnic facilities, and the opportunity to learn more about the battle that took
place on the grounds. In 1781, 70 patriots defeated a Tory force of more
than 400 men by sending a spy into their camp and launching a carefully
planned midnight attack.

WHITE LAKE

Before heading off to the coast, you might want to consider this beautiful
area for your family's annual vacation. Billed as "The Nation's Safest
Beach," **White Lake** offers all the amenities of a beach vacation, but it's

not on the coast. Just take Highway 701 north from Elizabethtown to get there. The lake is the largest of seven lakes known as the Bladen Lakes, which were formed by meteors that crashed into the earth more than 100,000 years ago. White Lake offers crystal clear waters with a lovely, white sandy bottom in addition to amusement rides, arcades, restaurants, and other commercial entertainment and activities. The cool fresh water is safer for kids because of the absence of the tides, currents, and unexpected depressions that are found at coastal beaches.

The area offers more than a dozen accommodations that include hotels, motels, cottages, and campgrounds. **Goldston's Beach,** one of the oldest recreation areas on the beach, was developed by local entrepreneurs, beginning at the turn of the century. It offers accommodations in apartments, cottages, and a motel. A bathhouse is available at the beach, as is a sandwich shop for a quick lunch. The kids will probably want to head to the arcade, too, or to one of the piers to get in a little fishing. For more information call the resort at (910) 862–4064. The **Crystal Beach Motel** (910-862-3660) can also provide accommodations for your stay, but the kids will be more interested in the more than twenty amusement rides nearby.

CALABASH

Now we can head to the coast. If you haven't discovered it before now, a visit to **Calabash,** located in the southeast corner of the state on Highway 17, is sure to become a family adventure tradition every time you come to this part of the coast. This small fishing community is the southernmost town in North Carolina and has become famous for the Calabash style of cooking seafood. Fish, shrimp, and other goodies are deep-fried to a golden brown and are usually served with hush puppies and coleslaw. More than thirty family-style restaurants line the streets of this quaint village, where fresh local seafood is delivered daily. In 1989, Calabash merged with the Carolina Shores golfing community, which includes not only some of the best courses in the Carolinas but a wide variety of specialty shops as well.

SUNSET BEACH

Accessible by a unique one-lane pontoon bridge, you'll quickly learn where this laid-back island just off the coast got its name. You'll feel almost

JIMS' TOP FAMILY ADVENTURES ON THE SOUTHERN COAST

1. Bald Head Island
2. North Carolina Aquarium, Kure Beach and Pine Knoll Shores
3. USS *North Carolina* Battleship, Wilmington

secluded if you decide you want to rent one of the large cottages situated behind the tall sand dunes on Sunset Beach. This little island, only 3 miles long, is the southernmost of three communities located on what are known as the Brunswick Islands. (The other two are Ocean Isle Beach and Holden Beach, which we'll get to next). A small cottage or apartment that accommodates four to six people will cost about $100 a night in season in this area (and along most of the coast). More extravagantly furnished, large houses cost between $1,000 and $1,500 per week. You can call the South Brunswick Islands Chamber of Commerce at (800) 426–6644 for information on accommodations and golf packages.

OCEAN ISLE BEACH

Ocean Isle Beach provides more surf, sand, and sunshine. This island is located just north of Sunset Beach. Here you can enjoy 7 miles of beaches and fish from the surf or pier. To get out on the ocean and try your fishing luck in deeper water, drop by **Pelican Pointe Marina and Dry Storage,** 2000 Somerset Road, or call (910) 579–6440. They offer full- and half-day fishing trips. If you'd like to try your hand at crabbing, it probably can be done just outside your back door. Everything you need is here on this island, including restaurants, specialty shops, a miniature golf course, and a water slide.

Whether you are at Ocean Isle for a day or a week, make it a point to stop by the **Museum of Coastal Carolina,** located on Second Street. You don't have to get wet to see the spectacular sites of local ocean life. Wall and floor murals give you a feeling of actually being in the water. The museum includes shark jaws, a huge seashell collection, displays of coastal animal life, and Civil War artifacts. Admission costs $3.00 for adults and $1.00 for children through age eleven. The museum is open from 9:00 A.M. to 5:00 P.M. Monday through Friday and 1:00 to 5:00 P.M. Sunday. Call (910) 579–1016 for more information.

You can call the town of Ocean Isle Beach at (800) 248–2504 to get information on accommodations.

HOLDEN BEACH

If beautiful sunsets and seclusion aren't enough to keep the kids entertained, give the largest and northernmost of the Brunswick Islands a try. The kids will love Holden Beach, which is easily accessible from Highway 74 if you're coming from the west. The 11 miles of beach have long been a favorite haunt of those who live to fish, but the area has grown to be more family oriented. It now includes amusements, arcades, and other commercial attractions. Call the town of Holden Beach at (901) 842–6488 for more information.

The **Festival By the Sea,** Holden Beach's biggest annual event, attracts people with its arts and crafts, parade, games, and entertainment. The festival kicks off the last Friday of October with a Halloween carnival for children and continues Saturday with road races, volleyball, sand sculpture contests, and kite-flying contests. A street dance is also traditionally held that night. Gospel singing is the center of attention on Sunday as the festival continues until dark. Call (910) 842–3828 for more information.

LONG BEACH

State Highway 211 will give you access to Oak Island, the location of three of North Carolina's most popular vacation communities: Long Beach, Yaupon Beach, and Caswell Beach. You can get more information on Oak Island by calling the Southport–Oak Island Chamber of Commerce at (800) 457–6964. You'll love the calm surf offered on the southern-facing islands. Long Beach is located in the geographic center of the island, making it the perfect central location for day trips in addition to fun on the beach. Here you'll be able to swim along 8 miles of beach, with fifty-two areas for public access and lifeguards at many marked locations. **Long Beach Cabana** features two fishing piers and a gazebo. The town also has a big arcade that includes a swimming pool as well as video games and billiard tables.

YAUPON BEACH

Yaupon Beach is the smallest of the three Oak Island resort communities, but it is a favorite for families who enjoy a friendly small-town atmosphere. It offers about 1 mile of beach, cozy family cottages, and the convenience of a number of golf courses and other recreational activities.

CASWELL BEACH

The third community on Oak Island is Caswell Beach. In addition to the gentle tides along the 4 miles of beach, here you will find the **Oak Island Lighthouse,** the nation's most modern, which opened in 1958. Also located on this beach is the Oak Island Coast Guard Station and **Fort Caswell.** Built in 1826, the fort is now owned by the North Carolina Baptist Assembly. The Civil War stone-and-earthen fort was abandoned in 1865 during a violent naval bombardment north of here. Today you can tour the remains of the fort and bunkers that remain there. For more information call (910) 278–9501.

SOUTHPORT

It's a short drive to Southport, located at the junction of the Cape Fear River, the Intracoastal Waterway, and the Atlantic Ocean. To get there, take State Highway 133 north from Yaupon Beach to State Highway 211 east. If your family enjoys sailing and deep-sea fishing, this is the place to go. But this port city, which is more than 200 years old, offers much more. You'll want to spend some time exploring the more than a dozen antique shops and take advantage of some of the exquisite dining available in the village. Call the Southport–Oak Island Chamber of Commerce at (800) 457–6964 for details.

The town is becoming famous for the **Southport Fourth of July Celebration,** which has become one of the state's largest annual celebrations, featuring games, contests, food, and, of course, fireworks.

A good educational afternoon trip is only about 2 miles north of town on State Highway 87. Take along a picnic lunch when you visit the **CP&L Visitor's Center** (910–457–6041). You'll want to allow about an hour to see the thirty hands-on displays on energy, electricity production, energy conservation, and nuclear power. Admission is free. The center is open from 9:00 A.M. to 4:00 P.M. Monday through Friday. From June through August it's also open from 1:00 to 4:00 P.M. Sunday. The center is closed New Year's, Thanksgiving and Christmas days.

Take Highway 87 north to Highway 133 and you'll find two other interesting attractions to round out your day trip. First, check out **Orton Plantation Gardens,** just off Highway 133. The plantation is surrounded by what once were rice fields that have now been converted into colorful gardens, bordered by live oak trees. The gardens are open daily. Hours from March through August are 8:00 A.M. to 6:00 P.M. and from September through November are 8:00 A.M. to 5:00 P.M. Admission costs $8.00 for adults, $3.00 for children six through eleven, and is free for those five and under. For more information call (910) 371–6851.

After you visit the gardens, head to the **Brunswick Town State Historic Site** just a few minutes away. Brunswick Town was the first capital of the colony of North Carolina and was a leading seaport during most of the eighteenth century. When you visit the museum at the site, you will see various artifacts and exhibits excavated from the remains of the original buildings, which were burned to the ground by the British in 1776. You'll also see the earthworks of Fort Anderson, built to help keep the Cape Fear River open for Civil War blockade runners, who shipped supplies to Confederate forces. It fell in 1865 during a fierce battle that also collapsed several other area forts. Markers have been erected to explain the history of the area. There is no admission fee. From April through October the site is open from 9:00 A.M. to 5:00 P.M. Monday through Saturday and 1:00 to 5:00 P.M. Sunday. From November through March it's open from 10:00 A.M. to 4:00 P.M. Tuesday through Saturday and 1:00 to 4:00 P.M. Sunday. For more information call (910) 371–6613.

BALD HEAD ISLAND

Bald Head Island is one of North Carolina's most exclusive and beautiful vacation resorts. You won't find any cars or even a bridge to this natural and historical area. To get here you must take a private yacht or catch the ferry at **Indigo Plantation and Marina,** off West Ninth Street in Southport. Security is provided at the twenty-four-hour parking lot at the marina. Daily trips to the island are made on the hour, from 8:00 A.M. to 6:00 P.M., except noon. Return trips to the mainland are made on the half hour, from 8:30 A.M. to 6:30 P.M., except 11:30 A.M. Cost to park your car is $4.00 per day, and the ferry ride costs $15.00 for adults, $8.00 for children ages three through eleven, and is free for children under the age of three.

Accommodations on Bald Head Island include two bed-and-breakfast inns that start at $125 per night during the summer, several condominiums that start at $250 per night during the summer, and homes starting at $325 per night during the summer. Whichever you choose, you'll find yourself on a vacation of luxury. All rental accommodations on the island come with fully equipped kitchens, washers and dryers, and one four-passenger golf cart. For more information on any of the attractions, or to make reservations, call the Bald Head Island information center at (800) 234–1666. Day trip packages are also available. One package, for example, costs $32 for adults, $27 for children three through twleve, and is free for children under three. It includes a two-hour historical tour, lunch, parking, and ferry fees.

In addition to fine dining, shopping, and relaxing by the pool or on the beach, you won't have any trouble finding ways to spend your time on this island of "sea oats, sand castles, and sunsets." **"Old Baldy,"** North Carolina's oldest lighthouse, built in 1817, marks the west side of Bald Head Island. Although its function has been replaced by the Oak Island lighthouse, the 110-foot tower is open for climbing. The Old Baldy Foundation, formed in 1985 and charged with maintaining the lighthouse, has been making plans to turn the lighthouse keeper's cottage into a museum. Admission is free, and hours vary. Call (910) 799–4640 to find out when it's open.

Most rental accommodation packages on the island include a temporary membership to the **Bald Head Island Club,** South Bald Head Wynd, which offers fine dining, live entertainment, a clubhouse, and a host of recreational facilities. Here you can enjoy the swimming pool, a challenging golf course, tennis courts, and croquet greenswards. Coaching for young and old alike is available for all these activities. The club offers a range of dining experiences, including elegant evening dining, a lunch grill, a cafe for casual dining, a delicatessen, and a snack bar by the pool.

Island Passage, at North Bald Head Wynd, offers a selection of sportswear and accessories. You can also get help in planning a number of different activities, such as clamming, crabbing, cycling, and canoe trips. Equipment for these adventures—as well as beach umbrellas, chairs, or even an extra golf cart—is available for rent.

Bald Head is a place for all ages. Children ages five to twelve will have a great time at **Camp Baldy,** which offers a wide variety of fun activities including hikes along the **Kent Mitchell Nature Trail.** The island is host to a number of interesting species of animals and plants. Here you may get a glimpse of a river otter, a raccoon, or even a deer or a gray fox. Various plants are labeled along the trail. Also at the camp, which operates most mornings from mid-June through late August, your kids will be treated to beach trips, pool games, and scavenger hunts.

In addition, the **Bald Head Island Conservancy** on Federal Road sponsors workshops for young people, including canoe trips, turtle walks, beach sweeps, and conservation programs. But the conservancy's biggest task is the preservation of the endangered loggerhead turtle. More than 30 percent of all the loggerhead turtle nesting sites recorded on the North Carolina coast are on this island. The Sea Turtle Nest Protections Project is responsible for monitoring the nesting of these endangered turtles and holds special programs about them.

You might want to plan your trip to Bald Head Island around one of the many special events planned throughout the year, beginning with the Easter sunrise service at "Old Baldy" and the annual Easter egg hunt. Your family can hunt for Blackbeard's buried treasure on Memorial Day. Or you can come out for the golf cart parade, sand castle competition, and family Olympic games on the July 4th weekend. Special celebrations are held on most other holidays, too.

KURE BEACH

You're sure to enjoy yourself on Pleasure Island. Its two communities are Kure Beach and Carolina Beach. From the north, the island is accessible by

Be sure to visit one of North Carolina's three aquariums along its coast, where the family can explore the world of the sea. (Photo by Mike Booher, courtesy Dare County Tourist Bureau)

car over the U.S. Highway 421 bridge. To get to Kure Beach from the south, you'll have to take the toll ferry from Southport to Fort Fisher. The cost of the scenic, thirty-minute crossing of the Cape Fear River is $6.00 for the average vehicle. Crossings begin at 8:00 A.M. and end at 7:00 P.M., year-round. They are less frequent in winter. Right away you'll find plenty to do here.

The first attraction you'll come to is the **North Carolina Aquarium,** one of three such aquariums on the North Carolina coast. Located on Highway 421, the aquarium is sure to draw your kids into the world of ocean life. Here they'll see a shark tank and get a chance to pick up a number of sea creatures at the touch tank. This aquarium also features a stingray exhibit, a turtle exhibit, a life-size whale sculpture, and an alligator pond. There are special educational programs including films and presentations at the aquarium, in addition to special field trips. Admission costs $3.00 for adults and $1.00 for young people ages twelve through sixteen. Kids eleven or younger get in free. The aquarium is open from 9:00 A.M. to 5:00 P.M. Monday through Saturday and 1:00 to 5:00 P.M. Sunday. Call (910) 458–8257 for more information.

Fort Fisher State Historic Site is your next stop on Highway 421. This was one of the Confederacy's last major strongholds during the Civil War. The site includes a monument commemorating the largest land-sea battle of the war, which was fought in January 1865. Also at the earthen fort, you'll see a reconstructed gun emplacement, and you can walk along an interpretive history trail. The fort's museum features displays on the Confederate defense system, dioramas, an audiovisual show, and war artifacts. Picnic facilities are also available. Admission is free. From April through October, the site is open from 9:00 A.M. to 5:00 P.M. Monday through Saturday and 1:00 to 5:00 P.M. Sunday. The rest of the year hours are 10:00 A.M. to 4:00 P.M. Tuesday through Saturday and 1:00 to 4:00 P.M. Sunday.

Kure Beach features a dozen charming hotels, motels, and inns to choose from. Or rent one of the many available cottages. The beaches here are generally uncrowded, but several areas have lifeguards on duty. In addition, the town's pier is conveniently located in the middle of town. Call the Cape Fear Coast Convention and Visitors Bureau at (800)

222–4757, or (800) 922–7117 if you're in North Carolina, for a list of accommodations in the Kure Beach area.

CAROLINA BEACH

Carolina Beach, just north of Kure Beach, offers a number of amenities for a fun-filled beach vacation, and it's about a twenty-minute drive south of Wilmington down Highway 421. It's full of a variety of natural areas, but Carolina Beach offers the thrill of water slides and amusement rides, too. The **Jubilee Amusement Park,** located on Highway 421 just after you cross the bridge from the north, offers just that sort of fun. At the park you'll find dozens of exciting rides including a Ferris wheel, a merry-go-round, go-carts, and water slides. You can either buy tickets for rides at 50 cents each or buy combination tickets that range in price from $8.95 to $11.95 for adults and $5.95 to $8.95 for children through age five. Hours vary according to weather and season. Call (910) 458–9017 for more information.

You'll find plenty of hotels, motels, and cottages for rent at Carolina Beach, but you can also camp at **Carolina Beach State Park,** located on the waterway on the west side of the island. You can fish here, but no swimming is allowed, although public beach access is only a few minutes away. The park is one of the world's few natural habitats of the Venus fly-trap, a unique carnivorous plant that traps and dissolves insects that land on its leaves. There are several nature trails in the park, and markers will help you guide your family through them. Picnic facilities are available during daylight hours. Campsite rental is $9.00 per night. For more information call (910) 458–7770.

About 10 miles north of Carolina Beach you can treat your kids to a trip to the **Tote-em-in Zoo,** 5811 Carolina Beach Road. The zoo includes more than one hundred different animals in five acres of forestlike surroundings. You'll see zebra, baboons, monkeys, exotic birds, a Siberian tiger, and Clyde the camel. The zoo has a gift shop and plenty of concessions as well. Two small museums feature mounted animals, fossils, arrowheads, and World War II memorabilia. The cost is $4.00 for anyone age eleven or older and $2.00 for children ages two through ten. The zoo is open during the spring from 9:00 A.M. to 4:00 P.M. daily and during the summer from 8:30 A.M. to 6:00 P.M. daily. Call (910) 791–0472 for more information.

WILMINGTON

Wilmington is the largest and fastest-growing city on North Carolina's coast and offers dozens of attractions for people of all ages. From the large historic downtown district to the Intracoastal Waterway, the city is full of arts, recreation, and just plain fun, whether you are here for a day or for a week. The Wilmington area has been home to myriad famous people, including NBA superstar Michael Jordan, television journalists David Brinkley and Charles Kuralt, singer Sammy Davis, Jr., and more. The city has come to be known as "Hollywood East." More than a dozen feature films have been made in the area, including *Firestarter, Ironweed,* and *Silver Bullet.* No tours are available at the North Carolina Film Studios, opened here by Dino De Laurintis in 1984. If you're lucky, however, you might find yourself with a chance to play as an extra or to meet a star from the "other Hollywood."

Check out the big guns on the USS North Carolina. *(Courtesy Battleship* North Carolina*)*

The most popular tourist attraction in Wilmington is the **USS *North Carolina* Battleship,** located across the Cape Fear River just west of downtown. Known as "The Showboat," the battleship was commissioned in 1941, served in all twelve major Pacific naval campaigns in World War II, and earned fifteen battle stars. It was the most powerful battleship in the world at the time. In 1961, the ship was carefully restored and today stands majestically as a memorial in honor of the nearly 10,000 North Carolinians who gave their lives during the war.

You will probably want to spend at least two hours exploring the ship's nine decks, including the mess deck and galley, sick bay, and engine room. The kids will be amazed at the size of the sixteen-inch guns that trim the deck. They certainly will want to take a peek through the captain's periscope for a view of downtown. A look at the barber shop and living quarters provides an interesting perspective on military life in the forties. Signs, pictures, and push-button tapes will guide you through the ship, but portable tape recorders are also available for rent. A picnic area and snack bar are located nearby. The memorial is open daily from 8:00 A.M. to sunset. Admission costs $5.00 for adults and $2.50 for children ages six to eleven. Call (910) 251–5797 for more information

Captain J. N. Maffitt Cruises, located at Riverfront Park at the corner of Market and Water streets, offers taxi rides to the memorial for $1.00. Rides run every half hour, except 11:30 A.M. and 3:30 P.M. You can also catch a boat there for an informative sightseeing cruise on the Cape Fear River. The kids will get the biggest kick if you hitch a ride on the stern-wheeler *Henrietta II.* This narrated tour takes you on trips down the river about 8 miles. It's a good way to get a look at the historic buildings and learn about the importance of the port town. Tours are offered at 2:30 P.M. Tuesday through Sunday, except in winter. An additional 11:00 A.M. cruise is offered during the summer. Tours, depending on which you catch, cost between $5.00 and $8.00 for adults and are $3.00 or $4.00 for children age twelve or younger. Call **Cape Fear Riverboats** at (800) 676–0162 for more information.

If you make it to Wilmington in the spring or summer, take the 5-mile scenic drive around **Greenfield Park and Gardens,** located south of the battleship on Highway 421. Greenfield Lake is the recreation center of the

180-acre park, but spend a little time cruising through the cypress and dog-wood trees. In the spring the park comes alive with color as azaleas and roses begin to bloom. At the lake you can bring along a picnic lunch, rent a canoe or paddleboat, or take a hike down the 4-mile walking trail. The park generally is open daily during daylight hours. Call (910) 341–7855 for more information.

Another educational afternoon trip to take if you're staying in Wilmington is to the **Moores Creek National Battlefield,** a thirty-minute drive north on Highway 210, off Highway 421. This site commemorates the first Revolutionary War battle fought in North Carolina in February 1776. Markers and monuments lead you through a self-guiding trail and help explain the battle. A visitor center includes a small museum with photos, an audiovisual program, and war memorabilia. The site is also a nice place for a picnic, and all facilities are free. In the summer the site is open from 9:00 A.M. to 5:00 P.M. Monday through Friday and 8:00 A.M. to 6:00 P.M. Saturday and Sunday. In winter it's open from 9:00 A.M. to 5:00 P.M. daily. Call (910) 283–5591 for more information.

Before you take on downtown Wilmington, you'll want to get hold of a guide map at the visitor center at the corner of Third and Princess streets or by calling (800) 222–4757. You either can take a riverfront walking tour or see most of downtown during a driving tour in a single day.

Certainly one of the first stops the kids will want to make is at the **Wilmington Railroad Museum,** at the corner of Red Cross and Water streets. Here you'll find that the railroad is almost as important as the river is in this port town. The museum features dozens of exhibits from the railroads, dating back to 1840, and model railroad displays. You can board a steam locomotive and a caboose outside the museum. Admission costs $2.00 for anyone age eleven or older and $1.00 for children ages six through ten. Tykes age five or younger get in free. The museum is open year-round from 10:00 A.M. to 5:00 P.M. Tuesday through Saturday and 1:00 to 5:00 P.M. Sunday. Call (910) 763–2634 for more information.

You can walk from the museum down Front Street to the **Cotton Exchange,** which features more than thirty unique restaurants and shops in well-preserved, turn-of-the-century buildings. The shops once served as warehouses for the former cotton company. Here you'll find specialty shops, clothing stores, and antiques. Most shops are open from 10:00 A.M. to 5:30 P.M. Monday through Saturday and 1:00 to 5:00 P.M. Sunday. Call (910) 343–9896 for more information. Parking is available nearby.

Next, spend some time exploring the historic homes scattered throughout downtown. From Water Street take Market Street to the **Burgin Wright House,** at the corner with Third Street. Built in 1770, the three-story home is an example of the gentleman's townhouse of the times. Its huge foundation is constructed of stone from the city's old jailhouse. As you walk through the home, you'll see a collection of lovely eighteenth-century furniture and decorations. Admission costs $3.00 for adults and $1.00 for children and students ages five through seventeen. The home is open from 10:00 A.M. to 4:00 P.M. Tuesday through Saturday, except July 4, Thanksgiving, Christmas, and New Year's days. Call (910) 762–0570 for more information.

The **Zebulon Latimer House** is located two blocks away at the corner of Orange and Third streets. The furniture in this home, built in 1852, is the original furniture that belonged to the prominent merchant and his family. While it isn't the oldest home in the area, it is unique because of its Italianate Revival construction. Admission costs $3.00 for adults, $1.00 for young people ages six through eighteen, and is free for children age five and under. Hours are 10:00 A.M. to 4:00 P.M. Tuesday through Saturday and 10:00 A.M. to 3:00 P.M. Sunday. The house is headquarters for the Lower Cape Fear Historical Society, which conducts tours of the homes in the historic district. Call the society at (910) 762–0492 for more information.

Your next stop is a cultural one, and just a few blocks down Orange Street. **St. John's Museum of Art,** located at the corner with Second Street, is a complex of three distinctive buildings dating back to the early 1800s. The museum's main attraction is a collection of three centuries of work by North Carolina artists. You can peruse collections of painting, Jugtown pottery, and sculpture, all of which were created in the state. In addition, the museum attracts collections from all over the world. The joy is that you never know what you'll find at the museum from trip to trip. Admission costs $2.00 for adults and $1.00 for young people ages six through sixteen. Children ages five or younger get in free. Hours are 10:00 A.M. to 5:00 P.M. Tuesday through Saturday and noon to 4:00 P.M. Sunday. For more information call (910) 763–0281.

Another one of Wilmington's big draws for families is the **Cape Fear**

Museum, 814 Market Street. A 21-foot scale replica of the Wilmington waterfront and a 31-foot diorama are only two of the literally hundreds of exhibits at this special museum. The museum tells the story of the region from prehistoric times to the present in "Waves and Currents: The Lower Cape Fear Story," a 600-square-foot exhibit that shows the development of this part of the coast. You'll also discover special interactive programs for children, videos, and more. Admission costs $2.00 for adults and $1.00 for students and children ages six or older. Kids age five or younger get in free. Hours are 9:00 A.M. to 5:00 P.M. Tuesday through Saturday and 2:00 to 5:00 P.M. Sunday. Many of the programs offered at the museum change from time to time, but you can call (910) 341–7413 for more information.

WRIGHTSVILLE BEACH

If you're heading from Wilmington to **Wrightsville Beach,** take an hour or so to visit **Airlie Gardens,** located just off Highway 74/76. The 5-mile scenic drive features extensive azalea and camellia plantings, truly a sight to behold during the month of April. You will also see a variety of rare evergreen trees, stately live oaks, well-kept lawns, and lakes as you make your journey through the park. Admission costs $6.00 for anyone age ten or older; children age nine or younger get in free. The gardens are open 8:00 A.M. to 6:00 P.M. daily in March and April and from 9:00 A.M. to 6:00 P.M. daily from May through October.

Wrightsville Beach is a family community that has become a popular meeting place for reunions or extended family vacations. It's quieter than most, and the beautiful white beaches have been well preserved. The area offers fine hotels, motels, apartments, and cottages. The village also offers a number of delightful restaurants and shops. Several piers and marinas will give you the opportunity for fishing, but if you come here you'll probably be charmed into just relaxing. Call the Cape Fear Coast Convention and Visitor Bureau at (800) 222–4757 for more details.

SURF CITY

You'll find that the beaches here on Topsail Island are still largely uncrowded, but you'll also discover many other fun things to do on this island, located midway between Jacksonville and Wilmington. The island got its name from merchant sailors who frequently saw pirates hiding in the marshes on the west side of the island. Tall foliage hid the ships, but the sailors could see the tops of the sails, hence the name Topsail (pronounced *topsil*) Island. Surf City is the commercial center of Topsail Island, but the beauty of the beaches has been well preserved. You get here by State Highway 50 from Highway 17. One of the last swinging bridges in North Carolina will take you across the Intracoastal Waterway.

While visiting much of North Carolina's coast, you may be surprised to wake up one morning to find that a loggerhead turtle has visited your beachfront cottage and nested there. The Topsail Turtle Project has been established to help protect this endangered species, which nests along Topsail Island's 26 miles of beach from May through August. Volunteers have established a **Loggerhead Turtle Exhibit** at town hall, on State Highway 210. The exhibit explains the life cycle of the turtle and includes nesting replicas and photographs. You'll also learn how to help preserve the animal. The exhibit is open from 8:00 A.M. to 5:00 P.M. daily. Call (910) 328–4131 for more information.

At the **Topsail Island Trading Company,** 201 New River Drive (910–328–1905), you'll find an interesting blend of gifts, beach supplies, and other goodies. Captain Ed, an entertaining mannequin playing the piano, will greet you and the kids. You'll want to try one of the more than thirty flavors of fudge and a big glass of freshly squeezed lemonade, too. The shop also stocks a healthy supply of North Carolina–made products from crafts to confections. Here you can also arrange a relaxing boat tour of the Intracoastal Waterway. *Kristy's Kruiser II,* a 33-foot pontoon boat, is ready to take you on 45- or 90-minute tours, where you're likely to see osprey, pelicans, egrets, and porpoises in their natural habitats. Forty-five-minute tours cost $10 per person and 90-minute tours $15 per person for anyone age two or older. Children age one or younger ride free. Trips leave at 2:00, 4:00, 6:00, and 8:00 P.M. Call (910) 328–8687 for more information on boat tours.

If you're in the mood for fresh local seafood, you won't have trouble finding a restaurant ready to serve it up. But for a tasty country-cooked meal take the short drive to Highway 17 and **Betty's Smokehouse Restaurant.** You can get seafood here, too, but you'll probably want to try the specialty—barbecue, chicken, or ribs. Betty's is open for breakfast, lunch, and dinner, from 6:30 A.M. to 10:00 P.M. daily. (It closes at 9:00 P.M. in winter.) Call (910) 329–1708 for more information.

Give the kids a treat at **Surf City Water Slide and Fun Park,** located at North Shore Drive and Greensboro Avenue. In addition to the water slide, you'll find several hours of entertainment at the game room. You can use the slide for $5.00 an hour or $10.00 for the day. Come and go as much as you like. The park is open during irregular hours according to the season and weather, so call ahead at (910) 328–2004 for hours and more information.

TOPSAIL BEACH

Topsail Beach is the southernmost community on Topsail Island. Accessible only from the north via Highway 50, it's the least crowded area, but there are two fishing piers and a quaint shopping district. Stop in at **Island Treasures,** a different sort of souvenir shop in a rustic building on the south end. It's a good place to browse for gifts or for the kids to pick up a game or water toy. The shop also features a Christmas corner and North Carolina art, pottery, and porcelain.

In the 1940s, Topsail Beach played a significant role in the origination of the U.S. space program. Tall, white concrete structures, used as observation towers during Operation Bumblebee, remain standing there. Operation Bumblebee was a secret U.S. Navy project that resulted in the development of the ramjet and technology that allowed human beings to break the sound barrier. These findings also led to the development of the U.S. space program and other advances in technology. The former test launchpad has been converted into a patio, and in 1993, the building where the test rockets were assembled was converted in the town's community center and a museum. You can visit the **Topsail Island Museum,** located in the community center at 720 Channel Boulevard, where the operation and the history of the island are explained. Videotapes, operation displays, and World War II artifacts help depict this island's history. Admission is free. The museum is open from April through October from 2:00 to 4:00 P.M. Saturday and Sunday. Call (910) 328–1038 for more information.

For a boat tour with a different twist, try **Topsail Belle Tours,** based at the Topsail Sound Pier on the waterway. On Monday, Wednesday, and

Friday the *Belle,* a 51-foot cruise vessel, departs at 9:30 A.M. for a shell-hunting excursion on deserted Lea Island. The trip costs $7.00 per person but is free for children age five or younger. Scenic tours are available on the *Belle* at noon, 2:00 and 4:00 P.M. The tours cost $7.00 for anyone ten or older and $3.50 for kids ages three through ten. Children age two or younger ride free. Concessions are available on board, but you can bring a cooler and other necessities for the shell-hunting trip. Call (910) 328–3641 for more information.

One of the most popular restaurants in Topsail Beach will be a big thrill for the kids. They'll love watching the cooks toss pizza dough at **Catalina Pizacco,** 718 South Anderson Boulevard. You can munch out on a huge 18-inch pie, or more adventurous eaters may like to try the zesty taste of gazpacho, a cold Spanish soup. The restaurant is open daily, but hours vary according to season. Call (910) 328–8447 for more information.

If just playing in the waves isn't enough for you, go by **Topsail Water Sports,** 1184 North Anderson Street. Here you find available for rent wave runners, jet skis, boogie boards, kayaks, and more. Hours are 9:00 A.M. to 6:00 P.M. daily. Call (910) 328–1141 for more information.

NORTH TOPSAIL BEACH

Head north from Surf City on Highway 210 and you'll find North Topsail Beach. This community is noted for natural diversity. It was once a separate island, but time slowly turned the sea into land. Now you'll find picturesque marshes, home to egrets, herons, and other graceful creatures, against a backdrop of dense maritime forests. Just minutes away are beautiful sand dunes and roomy beaches.

You will certainly want to stop by **Salty's Fishing Pier,** whether you fish or not. It's a great place for an evening stroll, to grab a quick snack, or to play video games. Kids age nine or younger fish free, and tackle is available for rent. The place is open twenty-four hours a day, seven days a week during warm months. Call (910) 328–0221 for more information.

SNEADS FERRY

Located on the mainland on Highway 172, Sneads Ferry is home to the **Annual Sneads Ferry Shrimp Festival.** Since 1971, the community has sponsored this two-day event, usually held the second weekend in August. Here the whole family will enjoy a parade, carnival, arts and crafts, historical displays, and, of course, lots of fresh shrimp. There is a $2.00 per person gate admission fee, and plates of shrimp cost $6.00 each. Call (910) 327–4911 for more information.

Head next to **Treasure Island Fun Park,** located on Highway 210 between Sneads Ferry and Old Folkstone roads. Here you'll find a full evening of activity that includes a round of miniature golf, bumper boats, "grand prix" racing, and much more. Hours of operation may vary according to season and weather. Rides for bigger people cost $5.00 each, kiddie rides cost $3.00 each. Golf costs $2.50 per person. Call (910) 327–2700 for more information.

JACKSONVILLE

Jacksonville is home to **Camp Lejeune,** a 110,000-acre U.S. Marine Corps base. There aren't any formal tourist attractions on the base, but you can get a glimpse of how the marines live and work by visiting the site. You'll need to present a valid driver's license, automobile registration, and proof of insurance at the information center on State Highway 24 to be admitted onto the base. (From Sneads Ferry take State Highway 172 north to Highway 24.) You'll want to take the kids to the **Beirut Memorial,** located just east of the camp on Highway 17. The large granite memorial was built in honor of the 268 American marines and sailors who were killed in the 1983 attack on the U.S. barracks in Lebanon. Along Lejeune Boulevard, each Bradford pear tree represents the loss of one life from U.S. involvement in Lebanon and in the 1983 U.S.-led invasion of Grenada.

SWANSBORO

You can leave Jacksonville by way of Highway 24 to get to the Swansboro and Cape Carteret areas. For a moving, unforgettable experience, take the kids to see *Worthy Is the Lamb,* presented each summer at the Crystal Coast Amphitheater. The theater is located just across the bridge from Swansboro. The two-hour play is an inspirational, musical drama that documents the life of Christ, from his mission to his crucifixion and resurrection.

The spectacular set, a replica of the city of Jerusalem, is placed in front of a gorgeous, natural backdrop—the scenic White Oak River, representing the Sea of Galilee. Tickets cost $11.00 for adults and $6.00 for children ages six through twelve. Children under five are free but might have trouble sitting through the production. Performances are roughly from June through August at 8:30 P.M. Thursday, Friday, and Saturday and in September at 8:00 P.M. Friday and Saturday. Call (800) 662–5960 to make reservations or for more information.

Also located a short drive and ferry ride from Swansboro is Bear Island and **Hammocks Beach State Park.** This isn't an expedition for softies. Bear Island's 892 acres constitute a naturally preserved area with huge shifting sand dunes, a maritime forest, and marshlands. Only primitive camping is allowed here, but you can bring supplies for a picnic and take a swim from the unspoiled beaches. If you want to take in the natural beauty of the island, the interpretive displays at the ferry dock will get you started on one of the nature trails. The ferry costs $2.00 for anyone age three or older and $1.00 for children age two or younger. Catch the ferry every half hour from 9:30 A.M. to 5:30 P.M. at the dock on Highway 24, about 4 miles south of Swansboro.

PINE KNOLL SHORES

From Swansboro, take Highway 24 to Highway 58. Just across the bridge is a long, slender island with tons of fun waiting. This small community is home to the **Theodore Roosevelt Natural Area** and the **North Carolina Aquarium,** one of three located along North Carolina's coast. The area is dedicated primarily to preservation, but you'll also find a hiking trail and observation towers. At the aquarium you'll dive deep into a sea of exhibits, programs, and a live, hands-on display. This aquarium features live loggerhead turtles, colorful fish tanks, and an open tank where the kids can pick up crabs and other sea creatures. It's okay—they won't hurt you. The aquarium also sponsors presentations on site and at various locations throughout the area. No admission is required for the natural area and trails, which are generally open during daylight hours. The aquarium admission costs $3.00 for adults and $1.00 for young people ages six through sixteen. Hours are 9:00 A.M. to 5:00 P.M. Monday through Saturday and 1:00 to 5:00 P.M. Sunday; closed Thanksgiving, Christmas, and New Year's days. Call (919) 247–4003 for more information.

Pirate Island Park, located just south of here, is a lot of fun. This family amusement park is good for a full afternoon of adventure, or plan to spend your evening hours here at the miniature golf course and video arcade. The park includes two giant water slides, two kiddie slides with a baby pool, and bumper boats as well. Hours vary according to season and weather. Call (919) 247–3024 for more information. Your best bet here is to pick one day and pay $11 each for all-day golf and all-day water sliding.

ATLANTIC BEACH

Although Atlantic Beach is a little more popular than some of the other beach communities on the southern coast, it's a good central location for active families looking to fill their vacation with day trips and other adventures. Atlantic Beach is host to a sand sculpture contest usually held the first weekend in May and the **Carolina Kite Flying Contest** in October.

A great place for families to stay is **Oceanana Family Resort,** on the oceanfront, several blocks from downtown. More homey than fancy, the resort features two- and three-bedroom apartments, a free breakfast of fruit and pastries served by the pool daily, and occasional watermelon parties. You can relax on the oceanfront lawn while the kids play on the playground. Basketball and volleyball courts are located on the property, and the pier is only a short walk away. In-season rates for a family of four start at around $95 per night. Call (919) 726–4111 for rates or other information.

Fun 'n Wheels Family Fun Park, located at the boardwalk downtown, really cranks up in the evenings. Here you'll find kiddie cars for younger children and racing go-carts for teens and older kids. You might also want to take your knocks on the bumper cars or bumper boats. The 55-foot Ferris wheel is a traditional beach thrill, but a more modern experience is the feeling of weightlessness in the amazing gyro. Fees are charged separately for each attraction. The park is open from noon to midnight daily from Memorial Day through Labor Day and on weekends only in April, May, September, and October. Ride fares range from $1.00 for a child nine and under to ride the Ferris wheel to $4.00 for a ride on the big go-carts. For more information call (919) 240–0050.

Fort Macon State Park, located at the east end of Highway 58, is one of the most popular attractions here. The fort is a massive, five-sided fortress constructed in 1826 to protect the region against foreign attacks, but it was seized from Union forces at the start of the Civil War. It changed hands several times over the course of the war, served as a federal prison for nearly a decade after the Civil War, and was garrisoned for use during World War II. Rangers present programs on a daily basis during vacation seasons, including a deafening musket-firing demonstration. They also conduct tours of the fort, or you can tour it yourself with the help of push-button tape and mannequin displays. Some parts of the fort, including the commandant's quarters, have been restored to their wartime condition. No admission is charged. The park, including picnic facilities and bathhouse, is open generally during daylight hours. The fort is open from 9:00 A.M. to 5:30 P.M. daily. Call (919) 726–3775 for more information.

MOREHEAD CITY

Just east across the bridge, on Highway 70 on the mainland, you come to Morehead City, a lovely waterfront community and the host of the **North Carolina Seafood Festival,** held the first weekend in October. Here you'll be treated to seafood galore and can enjoy the flounder-flinging contest, as well as live entertainment and plenty of games and activities for the kids. Activities are held mainly on the waterfront, but the county abounds with events, including sailboat and road races, and tennis and golf tournaments. Call (919) 726–6273 for more information.

Any time of year, be sure to see the **Carteret County Museum of History and Art,** 100 Wallace Drive in Morehead City. The museum is a potpourri of changing exhibits, ranging from native artifacts to vintage clothing to war items to shells, and more. Admission is free. The museum is open from 1:00 to 4:00 P.M. Tuesday through Saturday. Call (919) 247–7533 for more information.

BEAUFORT

A bridge allows Highway 70 to continue across the Beaufort Inlet from Morehead City to Beaufort. You'll want to spend some leisurely hours strolling the boardwalk in this picturesque waterfront town, or catch the big red double-decker bus for a tour of Historic Beaufort-by-the-Sea. **Historic Beaufort Bus Tours** will take you on a one-hour tour of North Carolina's third-oldest town, narrated by a guide dressed in clothes of the eighteenth century. The cost of the tour is $5.00 per person. Trips depart from **Beaufort Historic Site,** 138 Turner Street, at 11:00 A.M. and 1:30 P.M. Monday and Wednesday and at 11:00 A.M. Saturday from April through October. Call (919) 728–5225 for reservations.

If you can't catch a bus tour, guided tours and living history demonstrations are offered at the Beaufort Historic Site. You'll see weavers working on antique looms and more. The site is comprised of four homes built around the turn of the nineteenth century. The courthouse was built in 1796. The county jail was built in 1829; the apothecary and doctor's office were built about the same time and remained in use as late as 1933. All the buildings have been totally restored, and you'll see many of the authentic pieces of furniture and tools used at the time. Admission is $5.00 for adults, $2.00 for children six through twelve, and children under six are free. Guided tours are held at 10:00 and 11:30 A.M. and at 1:00 and 3:00 P.M. Monday through Saturday. Call (919) 728–5225 for more information.

The skill of the seafarers of yesteryear comes alive at the **North Carolina Maritime Museum,** 315 Front Street. The museum features full-size watercraft and displays that help you discover many of the mysteries of the sea. At the **Harvey W. Watercraft Center,** located across the street, you can see how these wooden boats were made, as skilled craftsworkers construct them in front of you. The museum also sponsors special programs throughout the year, including the Strange Seafood Exhibition and trips on a research vessel, where you can actually help collect and identify marine life. No admission is charged to the museum, but call ahead for information on special events and trips. The museum is open from 9:00 A.M. to 5:00 P.M. Monday through Friday, 10:00 A.M. to 5:00 P.M. Saturday, and 1:00 to 5:00 P.M. Sunday. It's closed New Year's, Thanksgiving, and Christmas days. Call (919) 728–7317 for more information.

Beware! Stay alert at all times on board the **Mystery Harbour Cruise Ship.** You never know when a pirate might come aboard the vessel as you tour the harbor near Beaufort. The ninety-minute cruise begins at Front Street and takes you past historic places, Blackbeard's house, and

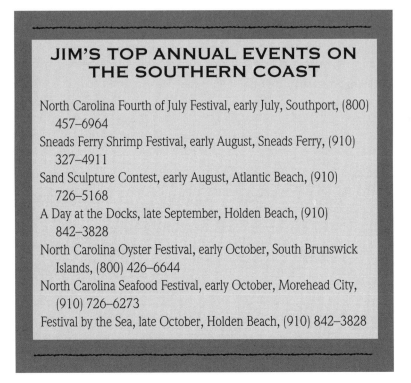

JIM'S TOP ANNUAL EVENTS ON THE SOUTHERN COAST

North Carolina Fourth of July Festival, early July, Southport, (800) 457–6964

Sneads Ferry Shrimp Festival, early August, Sneads Ferry, (910) 327–4911

Sand Sculpture Contest, early August, Atlantic Beach, (910) 726–5168

A Day at the Docks, late September, Holden Beach, (910) 842–3828

North Carolina Oyster Festival, early October, South Brunswick Islands, (800) 426–6644

North Carolina Seafood Festival, early October, Morehead City, (910) 726–6273

Festival by the Sea, late October, Holden Beach, (910) 842–3828

the natural sites on the nearby islands. Trips cost $8.00 for adults and $5.00 for children ages six through eleven. The narrated voyages are held three times daily from April through October. Call (919) 726–6783 for departure times or other information. The mystery ship also provides great half-day fishing trips that are ideal for children and beginners. Fishing on calm waters means seasickness won't be a problem, and all equipment is provided for you. The cost is $19.00 for anyone age eleven or older, $11.00 for children ages six through ten, and $6.00 for children age five or younger. Fishing trips begin at 8:00 A.M. and end at noon.

Sometimes you can see the wild ponies of **Carrot Island** grazing the shoreline from the Beaufort waterfront, but for a better look and to learn more you'll want to catch the ferry from Harpoon Willie's on Orange Street. Not only will you see the ponies, you can swim in the crystal-clear waters and hunt for shells along the white, sandy beach. The **Rachel Carson Estaurine Reserve,** which spans this chain of islands, offers occasional guided tours. Two-and-a-half-hour guided tours, which point out various aspects of nature and maritime heritage, are held in addition to the ferry trips. The ferry to Carrot Island costs $8.00 for adults and $4.00 for children age eleven or younger. Ferries leave every thirty minutes and run from 9:00 A.M. to 5:00 P.M. daily. Call (919) 728–6888 for more information.

CEDAR ISLAND

Your ferry to the Outer Banks leaves from the town of Cedar Island on the island of the same name, but you can also spend some time on horseback before you leave. **White Sand Trail Rides,** located near the ferry landing on Highway 12, is for children and adults, experts and novices. (It's about a forty-five-minute drive from Beaufort to Cedar Island. Take Interstate 70 north to Highway 12, which crosses a bridge onto the island.) Experienced parents can lead their children on a half-hour beach ride for $10 per person. Call (919) 729–0911 for more information.

HAVELOCK

Heading back to the west from Beaufort on Highway 101, you come to Havelock and the **Croatan National Forest.** Havelock is home to Cherry Point Marine Corps Air Station and is largely a retirement community. But you'll also find the 157,000-acre national forest bordering the Neuse River and home to deer, black bear, eagles, the endangered red-cockaded woodpecker, and a host of other creatures. The forest has a nice family campground, and you can hike, fish, and swim here. It's also home to the rare carnivorous Venus flytrap and several other rare plants. Sites and trails in the forest are generally open during the daylight hours April through October. All facilities are free except camping sites, which cost $5.00 per night. You can call the forest office at (919) 638–6528 for more information.

KENANSVILLE

West of the Croatan National Forest is North Carolina's heartland, which includes more farmland than anything else. You won't find a lot to do between Havelock and the small town of Kenansville, but the **Cowan**

Museum makes for a good stop while you're on the road. Traveling from Havelock to Kenansville takes about two hours taking Highway 17 from either Highway 58 or Highway 70. Take Highway 17 to Jacksonville and then take Highway 258 to Highway 24 west. Built in 1848, the Cowan Museum offers an interesting perspective on early American life. Hundreds of items, from tools to sewing machines, fill the museum's displays. Also on the grounds is a classic, one-room schoolhouse and a blacksmith's shop. Admission is free. The museum is open from 10:00 A.M. to 4:00 P.M. Tuesday through Saturday and 2:00 to 4:00 P.M. Sunday. Call (919) 296–2149 for more information.

Also on Highway 24, you'll find **Liberty Hall,** a plantation built for the Kenan family in the early 1800s. Here you can explore the main house, a restored example of antebellum architecture, where you will see two dining rooms (one for winter, one for summer), a wine cellar, and bedrooms, all of which have been fully furnished. You can also see the attached kitchen, carriage house, and smokehouse. Admission costs $4.00 for adults and $2.00 for children ages six through eleven. There is no charge for children age five and under. Interpreters provide guided tours of the grounds from 10:00 A.M. to 4:00 P.M. Tuesday through Saturday and 2:00 to 4:00 P.M. Sunday.

The Northern Coast

North Carolina's Northern Coast offers much more than the thrill of riding waves in the surf, an abundance of sunshine, and all the other amenities that come with a beach vacation. Here you'll also find rich history, intertwined with the present. The towns inland offer tours of majestic old homes and museums, while the islands in the area offer evidence of the early settlers' trials as they first began to settle the mysterious New World. At the turn of this century, coastal winds lured two brothers from Ohio to learn to fly. They are memorialized on Hatteras Island.

But don't forget to take advantage of the natural aspects of this area, where the land works in fragile balance with the sea. That sometimes angry sea threatens America's tallest lighthouse in this land of lighthouses. There is also a lot to learn about the ocean and the creatures that live in and around it. You'll find ample opportunity to observe nature and work with it through fishing and the educational programs available along the coast.

U.S. Highway 64, from Raleigh, is probably the easiest and most direct route to the Manteo and Nags Head areas. U.S. Highway 264 will give you a little different picture and is a more direct route to the Ocracoke area. Once you're here, finding your way around won't be much of a problem. U.S. Highway 17 runs the length of the coastal plain inland. State Highway 12 runs through the 75 miles of **Cape Hatteras National Seashore,** which includes the Ocracoke, Hatteras, and Bodie islands.

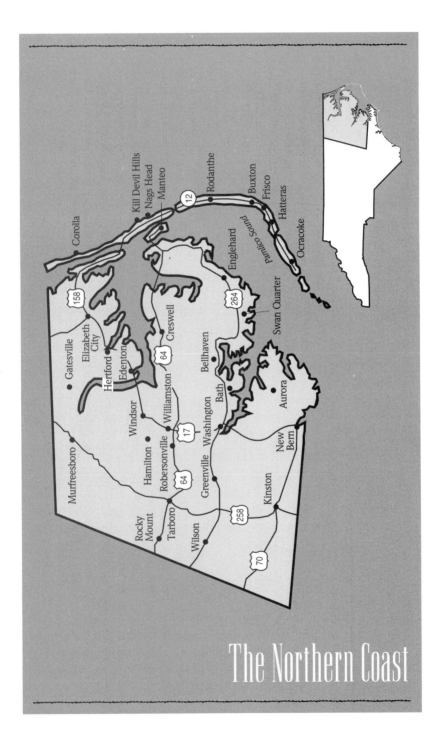

The Northern Coast

KINSTON

We'll start in the southern part of the Northern Coast region, at the intersection of Highway 17 and U.S. Highway 258, where you'll find Kinston. Part of North Carolina's Civil War heritage is told in Kinston, even though it's less than a heroic epic. In Kinston you will find the **CSS *Neuse* State Historic Site.** The *Neuse,* known as "the gunboat" locally, is a 158-foot ironclad ship that looks somewhat like a river barge. The Confederate Navy began construction on the boat in 1862, but it would never be completed. In March 1865, the Confederacy launched the boat in a hasty attempt to improve its faltering chances in the Civil War, but on March 12, the crew set fire to the ship and sank it to keep it from being captured by the enemy. A museum has been created on the grounds where the boat rests to tell about its history and the role this river town played in the Civil War. The museum includes a slide show and artifacts from the vessel.

Also on the site is the **Governor Caswell Memorial,** dedicated to Richard Caswell, the first governor of the independent state of North Carolina. He served in that post for six years and headed the committee that wrote the state constitution. You can see a sound and light show depicting the governor's life and visit his grave at the site, located at 2612 West Vernon Avenue (Highway 70 Business). From April through October, the site is open from 9:00 A.M. to 5:00 P.M. Monday through Saturday and 1:00 to 5:00 P.M. Sunday. From November through March, the site is open from 10:00 A.M. to 4:00 P.M. Tuesday through Saturday and 1:00 to 4:00 P.M. Sunday. Admission is free. Call (919) 522–2091 for more information.

NEW BERN

East of Kinston on Highway 70 at the junction with Highway 17 is where you'll find New Bern. New Bern is the picture of Southern hospitality, located on the scenic Trent and Neuse rivers. Settled in 1710 by German and Swiss colonists, it is North Carolina's second-oldest city and the state's first capital. The city features more than 150 historical landmarks, including **Tryon Palace Historic Site and Gardens** at 610 Pollock Street. Guided tours of the luxurious restored home of British Royal Governor William Tryon, built in 1770, are available from costumed guides. You and

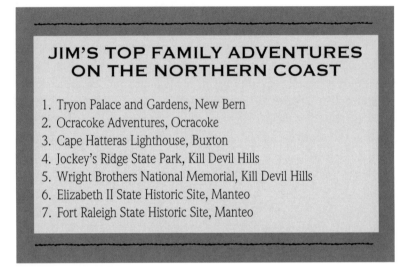

JIM'S TOP FAMILY ADVENTURES ON THE NORTHERN COAST

1. Tryon Palace and Gardens, New Bern
2. Ocracoke Adventures, Ocracoke
3. Cape Hatteras Lighthouse, Buxton
4. Jockey's Ridge State Park, Kill Devil Hills
5. Wright Brothers National Memorial, Kill Devil Hills
6. Elizabeth II State Historic Site, Manteo
7. Fort Raleigh State Historic Site, Manteo

your children will see not only the antiques and furniture that adorn the home, but you will enjoy the demonstrations on cloth making, candle making, blacksmithing and more.

Also part of the complex is the **Dixon-Stevenson House,** built in 1828 and decorated with furniture and antiques from the Federal and Empire periods. The **John Wright Stanly House,** built in 1783, also is part of the complex. The home has been furnished with pieces from that period, and the gardens have been designed like eighteenth-century English gardens. The complex is open from 9:00 A.M. to 4:00 P.M. Monday through Saturday and 1:00 to 4:00 P.M. Sunday. Admission costs $12.00 for adults and $6.00 for children six through seventeen. The tickets are good for all three homes, or you can buy tickets for each attraction separately. Call (800) 767–1560 for more information.

Even though you're not in San Francisco, you can take a trolley tour of New Bern's Historic District from Tryon Palace for an additional fee, or you can get a free walking map and continue to explore the city on your own. Catch the trolley or pick up a map at Tryon Palace. Trolley tours cost $10.00 for adults and $5.00 for children through age eleven.

New Bern offers what is billed as one of America's most in-depth private collections of Civil War memorabilia and weapons. Everyone in the family will want to visit the **New Bern Civil War Museum,** 301 Metcalf Street. In addition to the tons of weapons, the museum features the folding chair Ulysses S. Grant used in the field and an American flag with thirty-six stars. From April through October, the museum is open from 10:00 A.M. to 4:00 P.M. Tuesday through Sunday. Hours from October through March are 10:00 A.M. to 4:00 P.M. Saturday and Sunday only. Admission costs $2.50 for adults and $1.50 for children and students through age seventeen. Call (919) 633–2818 for more information.

The **Fireman's Museum,** 410 Hancock Street, features Civil War relics in addition to an extensive collection of early fire-fighting equipment. Original photographs have been preserved for the museum's displays and you also will be able to view old steam pumpers and other fire-fighting equipment used in the nineteenth century. Admission costs $2.00 for adults and $1.00 for children ages seven through twelve. The museum is open from 9:30 A.M. to noon and 1:00 to 5:00 P.M. Tuesday through Saturday and 1:00 to 5:00 P.M. Sunday.

AURORA

From New Bern take Highway 55 to Highway 306. Highway 306 North leads to the small town of Aurora and the **Aurora Fossil Museum,** at the corner of Fourth and Main streets. The museum tells the story of the coastal plain from the birth of the Atlantic Ocean to the present and features an unusual exhibit of life in the ocean fifteen million years ago. Here you can view dozens of fossils from the Miocene and Pliocene periods and even give fossil finding a shot yourself at a mound across the street. Summer hours are 9:00 A.M. to 4:30 P.M. Tuesday through Friday and 8:00 A.M. to 2:00 P.M. Saturday. Winter hours are 9:00 A.M. to 4:30 P.M. Monday through Friday. Admission is free. Call (919) 322–4238 for more information.

GREENVILLE

At Aurora, Highway 306 merges with Highway 33, which will take you west to Greenville, one of the largest cities in the coastal region. Here you will find plenty to do, whether your family is into the arts, history, or the outdoors. In Pitt County, you'll find twenty parks, six art galleries, a number of museums, and dozens of points of historical interest.

At the end of June each year, come out and see the stars—and find out how well they play golf. Greenville is host to dozens of festivals year-round, but the **Michael Jordan Celebrity Golf Classic** is one of the bigger draws. Basketball legend Jordan, other athletes, and entertainers join here to play in the benefit for Ronald McDonald Houses of North Carolina. It has become one of the area's biggest spectator events of the year. Even if you're not into golf, the kids might get a kick out of seeing pros from various other sports trying their hand at golf. For more information on the tournament call (919) 355–3222. The Greenville–Pitt County Convention and Visitors Bureau, at (800) 537–5564, can also give you details plus other information on the area.

One of the highlights you'll want to catch in Greenville is **River Park North,** 1000 Mumford Road, on the Tar River. Here you can fish, hike, and picnic year-round, and paddleboats are available on Saturday and Sunday when the weather is nice. The park is generally open during daylight hours. While at-the park, stop in at the **Adventures in Health Children's Museum,** a hands-on exhibit that focuses on anatomy and physiology. For example, one exhibit, designed to teach about stress, puts you in a cubical with flashing lights and then your stress level is tested. A second cubicle has been designed to help relax you and bring your stress level back down. Designed to promote healthy lifestyle choices, the museum also dedicates some time to safety and emergency preparedness. Admission is free. The museum is open from 1:00 to 5:00 P.M. Tuesday through Sunday from November through February and 1:00 to 6:00 P.M. from March through October. The park generally is open during daylight hours. You can call the park at (919) 830–4561 or the museum at (919) 752–7231.

The park is also home to another museum, the **Science and Nature Center.** Here the kids will love looking at the displays of African animals, colorful butterflies, and huge mammals. Also a big draw is the live reptile display. Admission costs a mere 25 cents per person. Center hours during March through October are 1:00 to 6:00 P.M. Tuesday through Sunday. Hours from November through February are 1:00 to 5:00 P.M. Tuesday through Sunday. Call (919) 830–4561 for more information.

WASHINGTON

From Greenville, catch Highway 264 east to the city of Washington. "The Original Washington," named in 1775 for the George who would become the first president of the United States in 1789, might prove the perfect quiet stopping point before or after a trip to the beach. Many of the buildings here on the waterfront have been renovated but aren't open to the public. A number of them have been converted into shops and restaurants if you're interested in a quiet day of shopping. The City of Washington provides a map of its historic district for walking tours. Call (919) 946–6194 for more information about Washington and Beaufort County.

While many of the bed-and-breakfast inns here have minimum age requirements for children, **Whichard's Beach Marina Campground** offers adventure for the whole family. Located a mile south on Highway 17 along the Pamlico River, the campground offers beaches, a marina, a game room, a water slide, and more. Call (919) 946–0011 for more information.

BATH

Just a few miles east of Washington on State Highway 92, you come to contemporary Bath and **Historic Bath,** North Carolina's first town, settled in the late seventeenth century and incorporated in 1705. Here you can tour the **Palmer-Marsh House,** which features one of Santa Claus's favorite stopping points—a 17-foot-wide chimney. The **Van Der Veer House,** built in 1795, features a gambrel roof and houses trinkets and other items that highlight the town's three centuries of history. **Saint Thomas Church,** the oldest church in North Carolina, is also part of the historic district. It has walls that are more than 2 feet thick. A nice place for a picnic is on the waterfront, located nearby on Front Street. Tours of the town and homes are conducted from April through October, from 9:00 A.M. to 5:00 P.M. Monday through Saturday and 1:00 to 5:00 P.M. Sunday. Historic Bath is open the rest of the year from 10:00 A.M. to 4:00 P.M. Tuesday through Saturday and 1:00 to 4:00 P.M. Sunday. Admission costs $1.00 per house for adults and 50 cents for children age eleven or younger. You can get more information on Historic Bath at the visitor center on Carteret Street or call (919) 923–3971.

Goose Creek State Park, located just west of Bath on Highway 92 along the Pamlico River, offers primitive camping, hiking, fishing, swimming, other outdoor activities, and nature programs. Two boardwalks let you actually walk out into the swamp and marsh, where oak trees are draped with Spanish moss. The park is open during daylight hours. Admission is free. Call (919) 923–2191 for more information.

BELLHAVEN

Do your kids collect things? If they do, they will get a kick out of the **Bellhaven Memorial Museum.** Located in Bellhaven city hall at 201 East Main Street, this museum grew out of a collection begun by Mrs. Eva Blount Way at the turn of the century. It started with her collection of 30,000 buttons but has grown to include coins, shells, war memorabilia, tools, and more. The museum is open from 1:00 to 5:00 P.M. daily. Admission is free. Call (919) 943–3055 for more information. To reach Bellhaven from Bath, simply head east on State Highway 99.

SWAN QUARTER

Continuing east from Bellhaven on Highway 264 takes you through **Swan Quarter National Wildlife Refuge,** 15,500 acres of salt marsh and woodlands bordering Pamlico Sound. Fishing is allowed at Bell Island from a 1,100-foot pier, but you and the kids might be more interested in just sitting back and watching. The refuge is host to a number of migratory birds that can be seen here; including terns, black ducks, brown pelicans, and loons. The refuge is open year-round during daylight hours. Call (919) 926–4021 for more information.

ENGLEHARD

A more popular stopping point is the **Mattamuskeet National Wildlife Refuge,** farther east on Highway 264 near Englehard. The 50,000-acre refuge includes Lake Mattamuskeet, the largest natural lake in North Carolina, averaging only 2 feet in depth. It is 18 miles long and 5 to 6 miles wide. The refuge provides protection for migratory birds, such as ducks, geese, tundra swans, and occasionally a bald eagle. Fishing and crabbing are allowed at the lake and adjacent canals during the spring, summer, and fall. During the winter the refuge is home to birds that migrate from as far away as Canada. Call (919) 926–4021 for more information.

OCRACOKE

Now we'll jump across the Pamlico Sound to the Outer Banks, starting with Ocracoke Island. You can get to the village of Ocracoke by ferry from Swan Quarter or Cedar Island. Crossing time is more than two hours, and the cost is $10 for the average vehicle. Reservations for toll ferries are recommended and can be made thirty days in advance. For a complete ferry schedule or to make reservations, call (800) 293–3779. The ferries on longer routes such as these are fairly comfortable and include air-conditioned lounges, complete with snack machines. The kids will probably want to spend some time on the sun deck to take in spectacular views of the islands and the shrimpers who will be hard at work.

At Ocracoke, State Highway 12 runs up the length of the island. Although it is quiet in Ocracoke, your family will love this charming village on the southern tip of the island. The island, which is 16 miles long, is home to just 700 people, many of whom still carry an Elizabethan accent in terms like hoigh toid for "high tide."

By the time you get to Ocracoke Village you'll find the narrow streets —lined with countless shops, restaurants, and inns—fairly crowded during the summer months. The aura of Ocracoke is enhanced by the oak and cypress trees with Spanish moss hanging from their limbs. But don't worry about the crowds; you'll find plenty of room to stretch out north of the village. Before you get to Ocracoke you will want to have a walking map, available on the ferries and at the National Park Service Visitor Centers located at the ferry docks. You'll find more than a dozen hotels, several bed-and-breakfast inns, and rental cottages that are available. For general information on the village, call the Ocracoke Civic and Business Association at (919) 928–6711.

A fun way to see the village and most of the island is by bicycle. The **Slushy Stand,** on the corner of Highway 12 and Silver Lake Road, provides more than just a quick snack. Here you can rent bikes for adults and children for $4.00 per hour or $12.00 per day. If you're ready to hit the beach, you can also rent umbrellas, chairs, and boogie boards. **Ocracoke**

Adventures (919–928–7873) can help you plan your trip. They provide family activities, guided tours, and more.

Travel north on Highway 12 to find **Beachcomber Campground.** Reservations for the oceanfront campground, 3 miles from the village, can be made through Ticketron outlets, or call (919) 928–4031. The campground gets you away from the hustle and bustle of tourists and is very scenic and nicely kept. Tent sites are $15 per night, and camper sites with hookups are $18 per night.

Active families will find a lot to do on Ocracoke Island. Those who like horses will want to get in touch with **Seaside Stables,** which provides scenic horse rides on the beach from June through August. Call (919) 928–3778 for information on rates and hours of operation. If you want to take the family fishing but don't have much experience, **Fish Tale Fishing Charters** is ready for a voyage through calm waters and to help the landlubbers who make their way here. It offers two- and four-hour fishing trips especially geared for families and children. They have all the equipment you need, and they will help you with the kids and teach them about their catch. Activities such as these start at around $20 per person and generally last a half day. Call (919) 928–3403 for rates or to make reservations.

If you don't plan to spend some time taking in the history of this island, you'll miss a lot of the charm it has to offer. You'll want to see the **Ocracoke Lighthouse** on Point Road west of the village. Built in 1823, the lighthouse is the state's oldest still in operation. Its beam that shines at night can be seen from 14 miles away, but it's not open for climbing.

Teach's Hole on Back Road is a pirate specialty shop that includes an exhibit about one of the island's most famous visitors—Edward Teach, also known as Blackbeard the Pirate. He was killed in a battle near the island by the British Royal Navy in 1718. Some say his treasure is still buried on the coast. A self-guided free tour depicts the escapades of the swashbuckler and his companions. The shop is open from 10:00 A.M. to 6:00 P.M. Monday through Saturday and 10:00 A.M. to 1:00 P.M. Sunday. Call (919) 928–1718 for more information.

North on Highway 12 are the **Banker Ponies.** These horses ran wild on the island until the late 1950s, when they were penned at their current home. The small horses are descendants of horses brought to the New

World by Spanish explorers as early as the sixteenth century and can be viewed and photographed from an observation deck just off the highway.

HATTERAS

By the time you get to the northern portion of Ocracoke Island, where the **Cape Hatteras National Seashore** begins, you'll find that the major attraction here is the sun, sand, and unspoiled beauty. The seashore is more undeveloped than any other portion of the Atlantic Coast, but a visit to any one of the villages here provides ample opportunity for educational and adventurous day trips. The free Ocracoke ferry takes you across Ocracoke Inlet to Hatteras Island, the central island in the Outer Banks. Highway 12 continues up the length of the island.

With the Gulf Stream only about 12 miles from the islands, fishing is ideal offshore from Hatteras, a quiet community on the southern tip of Hatteras Island. Fishing charters are available from a number of fishing centers in the area, or you might try your luck fishing from the pier located a few miles north of the village.

Off the coast of Hatteras Island are the dangerous Diamond Shoals, a bank of shifting sand ridges beneath the sea. They have been blamed for helping to sink more than six hundred ships in the area, earning Hatteras the nickname "Graveyard of the Atlantic." Some of the sunken ships are visible from shore, depending on tides and the shifting sand. Much of Hatteras Island is untamed and uncrowded. You might want to take some time for a quiet walk on the beach or just take in the scenery.

Four camping areas are available along the Cape Hatteras National Seashore on a first-come, first-served basis. All of these National Park Service facilities have showers, rest rooms, tables, drinking water, and grills, but no utility hookups. Rates start around $10 per night. You can get more information on the entire Cape Hatteras National Seashore by calling (919) 473-2111.

FRISCO

Push on north up Highway 12 just a little farther and you come to another of the island's tiny villages, Frisco. Here you will want to stop and visit the **Frisco Native American Museum and Natural History Center.** The museum features authentic collections of ancient artifacts, and the center features a nature trail, exhibits, a pavilion, and a picnic area. Admission is free, but donations are accepted. The center is open from 11:00 A.M. to 6:00 P.M. Tuesday through Sunday. Call (919) 995–4440 for more information.

BUXTON

Now get ready to climb. Buxton, farther north on Highway 12, is the home of the tallest lighthouse in the United States. At 208 feet, the **Cape Hatteras Lighthouse** is an international symbol for the North Carolina Coast and has gained more national attention over the past decade. Erosion from the treacherous sea began to threaten the lighthouse, and in the mid-1980s plans were undertaken to save it. Sandbags lining the sand dunes have slowed the erosion, and officials have planned to move the lighthouse farther inland. You can still climb the 268 steps to the top of the lighthouse and get a spectacular view of the surrounding area from outside. Children must be old enough to make the climb on their own. On the grounds of the lighthouse is the **Cape Hatteras Visitors Center and Museum.** Admission to both is free. They are open generally from 8:00 A.M. to 5:00 P.M. daily, year-round. For more information call (919) 995–4474.

RODANTHE

About 30 miles north on Highway 12 is one of North Carolina's oldest lifesaving stations. The **Chicamicomico US Lifesaving Service Station** was established in 1874, and the villagers who have volunteered here have been credited with saving the lives of hundreds of sailors who found themselves caught in fierce winter and tropical storms. Re-enactments of such rescues are performed weekly at the station during summer months. Admission is free, but the station continues to be renovated, so call for the hours it is open at (919) 987–2203.

Just north of Rodanthe begins the 5,915-acre **Pea Island National Wildlife Refuge.** You can use the observation platforms located throughout the area to view hundreds of species of local birds and any number of birds migrating to and from the refuge. It also has a visitor center and nature trail and sponsors bird walks and children's programs during the summer and fall. The refuge center is open during daylight hours, and programs are free. Call (919) 473–1131 to learn more.

If the kids are ready for a little bit of modern adventure, try **Waterfall Action Park.** It's one of the area's largest fun parks and includes water slides, race cars, kiddie cars, miniature golf, bumper boats, and more. Each attraction costs $6.00, or you can buy combination tickets, starting at $10.00. It's open May through September, but hours may vary. Call (919) 987–2213 for details.

After you cross the bridge across the Oregon Inlet, still on Highway 12, you move out of the largely unpopulated areas and into a more traditional tourist area. Bodie Island begins in the south at Coquina Beach, home of the **Bodie Island Lighthouse.** A visitor center, exhibits, and nature trail are open during daylight hours from May through September, but the lighthouse, built in 1872, is not open to climb. Call (919) 473–2111 for more information.

From Highway 12 you can see the **Laura Barnes Shipwreck of 1921.** It is one of the few shipwrecks that is usually visible. The 120-foot ship, one of the last sailing schooners built in America, ran aground during a storm. A swimming area and a picnic area are available nearby.

MANTEO

At Whalebone, Highway 12 encounters Highway 64, which crosses Roanoke Sound west onto Roanoke Island. You may want to take this twenty-minute side trip into the late sixteenth century before continuing north to the popular Nags Head resort area. In Manteo there is plenty to fill a day and evening, or even several days and evenings. Roanoke Island is the site of the earliest English settlements sent by Sir Walter Raleigh beginning in 1584. There is a lot here that depicts the lives of those settlers and others who helped shape the New World.

Coming from Highway 64 your first stop might be the *Elizabeth II* **State Historic Site.** The ship is a replica of the sixteenth-century sailing ship that brought some of the first settlers to America. Your kids will love striking up conversations with the interpretive guides dressed as sailors who work for Queen Elizabeth. They stay in character for the year 1585, so comments about television or cars won't be understood. After you tour the small vessel, you'll want to see the living history camp a short walk away. It's 1585 here, too, folks. You might find the queen's sailors whipping up a meal or crafting tools or preparing food for winter storage. The site is open from 10:00 A.M. to 6:00 P.M. daily, April through October, with the last guided tour at 5:00 P.M. It costs $3.00 for adults and $1.50 for children. For more information call (919) 473–1144.

After your visit to the *Elizabeth II,* journey through the quaint waterfront village on Roanoke Sound. At the **Waterfront Shops,** 207 Queen Elizabeth Avenue, you can take your time and explore the many unusual shops and restaurants, where you can find lunch or dinner. At the **Candle Factory** (919–473–3813) you can watch craftworkers produce candles in the shape of seashells, lighthouses, and more. Many more shops in the village will take you back in time. **Island Nautical** (919–473–1411) carries a large supply of nautical antiques, clocks, books, and decorations. You'll also find ship models and do-it-yourself kits. Most shops are open daily.

At the nearby Pirate's Cove Yacht Club you can catch a sight-seeing cruise aboard the ***Virginia Dare.*** The air-conditioned yacht leads you on a narrated trip through these historical waters. You'll hear a lot about the rich history of the area, including pirates who roamed the waters, early settlers, and the initial efforts at flight, while also learning about the natural features of the sound. The cost of the one-and-a-half-hour tour is $10.00 for adults and $6.00 for children through age eleven. Cruises run from mid-May through mid-October at 11:00 A.M. and 3:00 and 7:00 P.M.. The evening tour departs at 6:00 P.M. after Labor Day. Call (919) 473–9858 to make reservations or for more information.

Next, take a jaunt on Airport Road, 3 miles north of Highway 64, to the **North Carolina Aquarium.** It's one of three such aquariums on the coast. In addition to the displays of marine life and a touch tank, the aquarium offers special programs and educational films throughout the year. At this aquarium you'll see sharks, alligators, and coastal environmental displays. Admission to the aquarium is $3.00 for adults, $1.00 for young people ages six through sixteen, and free for children age five or younger. The aquarium is open from 9:00 A.M. to 5:00 P.M. Monday through Saturday and 1:00 to 5:00 P.M. Sunday; closed on Thanksgiving, Christmas and New Year's days.

Just past the aquarium you will find the Manteo Airport and **South-east Air Tours.** They offer three tours, ranging from $15 to $35 per person, and even a chance to take the controls yourself. One tour flies you over to the Outer Banks to Kitty Hawk and over the Bodie Island Lighthouse. The second trip offered also takes you over Oregon Inlet and Roanoke Sound. The third tour goes farther north to the unspoiled beaches of Duck and Currituck Sound. Call (919) 473–3222 for more information.

When you leave Airport Road, take a left on Highway 64, and on the right you'll see **The Christmas Shop.** Here at the Outer Banks' original Christmas shop you can choose from among thousands of ornaments. The shop also carries gifts, toys, candy and other yuletide yummies. The shop is open year-round. Call (919) 473–2838 for hours.

What was that next to the Christmas Shop—a cat house? Yes, but it's okay; the kids can go in there. **Janine's Cat House** is a cat lover's dream —a boutique designed especially for cat fanciers. They have cat cups, cat posters, cat jewelry, cat furniture, and more. At Janine's you can find just about anything you need to make your feline or the feline lover you know happier. You can call Janine's at (919) 473–1499.

Back on Highway 64, it's on to **Fort Raleigh National Historic Site.** The site includes a visitor center with exhibits of artifacts from the original site constructed in 1585. The center features the Elizabethan Room adorned with the paneling and fireplace from a sixteenth-century home, representative of the style of house in which the colonists lived. At the center you can also see a film on the attempts to establish the colonies and displays on colonial life. In addition, the National Park Service reconstructed the small earthen fort here in 1950 at the same location it was originally built in 1585. Many of the artifacts, including a wrought-iron sickle and Indian pipe excavated from the site, are on display at the center. Park interpreters present programs and special events at various locations of the site throughout the year. The site is open year-round. Admission to the fort and center is free. You can reach the park office at (919) 473–2111.

Plan to spend an hour or so wandering through the **Elizabethan Gardens,** located at the national historic site. Visitors entering the gardens through a replica of a Tudor gatehouse are led through myriad herbs, flowers, shrubs, water fountains, and trees. The gardens are open from 9:00 A.M.

to dusk daily. Admission to the gardens is $3.00 for adults. Children through age eleven are admitted free of charge. For more information on the gardens call (919) 473–3234.

Your trip to Manteo won't be complete without seeing **The Lost Colony** outdoor drama, which plays on the waterfront on the grounds of Fort Raleigh. Children and adults alike will be enthralled as the 150-member cast re-creates through drama, song, and dance the events leading to the mysterious disappearance of the men, women, and children who came here from England in 1587. Written by Pulitzer Prize winner Paul Greene, *The Lost Colony* opened in 1940 and has been playing ever since. The play also commemorates the birth of Virginia Dare, the first European child born in the New World, who disappeared along with the other colonists. Exactly what happened to them remains a mystery. The two-hour production is presented from early June to late August at 8:30 nightly,

It's a long climb to the top of the largest sand dune on the east coast at Jockey's Ridge State park. (Photo by Mike Booher, courtesy of the Dare County Tourist Bureau)

except Saturday. Weather changes rapidly on the waterfront, so bring along a jacket as well as bug repellent to keep the mosquitoes away. Tickets are $12.00 for adults and $6.00 for children through age eleven. For reservations call the box office at (800) 488–5012.

Darrell's Seafood Restaurant (919) 473–5366, less than a ten-minute drive from the theater on Highway 64, is a good place to eat before the show. The family-style restaurant features Darrell's specialty—grilled marinated tuna—but the menu also includes a healthy portion of local catches, a good children's menu, and baskets for light eaters. Darrell's is open for lunch and dinner, Monday through Saturday.

The Lost Colony Children's Theater also presents other special productions for children who might not be able to make it through the evening show. These are performed at various locations on the Outer Banks throughout the season. Call the Lost Colony Box Office for times, locations, and ticket prices.

NAGS HEAD

A little farther north from Whalebone, where you sidetracked to Manteo, on Highway 12 is Nags Head, where you'll find more of what you expect from a standard tourist center. Hotels, vacation cottages, and condominiums line the strip between the beach and Highway 12. You have plenty of attractions, amusements, and eateries to choose from here. Until you get to Nags Head, the islands often aren't wide enough to accommodate much more than the highway, but this broader area is able to accommodate an array of services, including major retail chain stores. Here you also get a fair share of water parks, water slides, miniature golf courses, and gift shops. Any number of beachfront accommodations are available, and the Dare County Tourist Bureau (800–446–6262) will provide you with a listing of these accommodations. Nags Head is a good central location if you are planning to stay a week or more in the area. Not only can you enjoy the sand, sun, and surf, there's simply a lot to do, rain or shine.

For the ultimate family adventure you might want to check in with **Kitty Hawk Kites,** just off Highway 12 on U.S. Highway 158, which also has outlets at Avon, Duck, and Corolla. They offer lessons in kayaking, windsurfing, and hang gliding as well as kites and kite supplies. Even

Take the family to see The Lost Colony *for an unforgettable experience. (Photo by Mike Booher, courtesy of the Dare County Tourist Bureau)*

young children can be accommodated in kayaking tours, but you must weigh at least 80 pounds to take hang-gliding lessons. Kayaking tours start at around $30 per person while other lessons start at about $15 per hour. Call (800) 334–4777 to make reservations or to learn more.

If hang gliding is a little too adventurous for your family, it's almost as much fun to sit back and watch at **Jockey's Ridge State Park.** This is the site of the largest sand dune on the East Coast, located on Highway 158. Most people come here to climb the 140-foot dune, while others come to fly kites in the wide-open, 414-acre park. Walking across the vast white sand almost makes you feel like you're walking across the desert. Picnic facilities also are available. Like most state parks, it is open during daylight hours, and admission is free. Call (919) 441–7132 for more information.

If you need to cool off after the climb, drop in at **How Sweet It Is** for a big scoop of homemade ice cream, right across the street from the park. The shop also has sandwiches and features an old-fashioned soda fountain. The shop's hours are generally 10:00 A.M. to 9:00 P.M. daily, but may vary according to season. Call (919) 441–4485 for more information.

Any time is a good time to try out your fishing luck on the **Nags Head Pier,** one of the oldest and longest on the Outer Banks. Tackle is available for rent, as is a cleaning station. The **Pier House Restaurant** serves three meals a day at reasonable prices. Treat the family to tasty local seafood in a casual dining atmosphere with an oceanfront view. You can also grab a home-style breakfast, beginning at 6:00 A.M.; spend the day fishing; and let them cook up your catch just the way you like it, for around $5.00. The pier is open twenty-four hours a day in spring, summer, and fall. The restaurant closes briefly between 4:00 and 5:00 P.M. but then remains open until 10:00 P.M. You can reach the pier at (919) 441–5141.

KILL DEVIL HILLS

This is where human beings learned to fly. On December 17, 1903, two bicycle shop owners from Dayton, Ohio, named Orville and Wilbur Wright took the first powered flying machine on a sustained flight. They kept the machine aloft for fifty-nine seconds and traveled 852 feet. Today, the **Wright Brothers National Memorial,** on Highway 158 north of Kill Devil Hills, stands on the same spot as a tribute to their accomplishment. It includes a museum on the history of flight and a demonstration of the principles they used, which are still instrumental to modern flight. Reproductions of the brothers' glider and the 1903 airplane are on display, and you will want to check out the reproduction of their camp workshop and hanger. Admission to the park, which is open daily, is $4.00 per vehicle. The memorial is open from 9:00 A.M. to 7:00 P.M. daily from mid-June through Labor Day and 9:00 A.M. to 5:00 P.M. the rest of the year; closed Christmas Day. Call (919) 441–7430 for more information.

Kitty Hawk Aero Tours offers a chance to take a flight from the same place the Wright brothers made so many attempts in their quest to fly. Their tour, which costs between $19 and $24 per person, flies over Oregon Inlet to observe the ocean life that includes sharks, porpoises, and sea turtles. They also fly you over the Bodie Island Lighthouse and Jockey's Ridge. Open cockpit planes are available, too. You can call them at (919) 441–4460.

After that, it's off to learn a little bit about one of nature's more unusual offerings at **Nags Head Woods Ecological Preserve,** where freshwater pools have bubbled up to create this 1,100-acre protected wetland. Access to the preserve is located off Highway 158 on West Ocean Acres Drive. Walking trails and displays provide an interesting look at one of the last and most diverse forests on the islands. The 1,100 acres of woodlands include dunes adjacent to a majestic hardwood forest. The staff presents guided tours and educational programs that explain the diversity of the area throughout the year. Admission to the preserve is free, but some programs may require a fee. Call (919) 441–2525 for more information.

The Promenade, on Barlow Road near the Wright Brothers Memorial Bridge, has dozens of activities for the entire family. The Promenade is a thirty-acre entertainment park with everything from golf to water sports, yet it isn't a traditional entertainment center in that it offers more peaceful surroundings. The eatery includes a coffee and draft house as well as ice cream and other snacks. You'll find a driving range, grass putting greens, a playground, and opportunity for kayaking or other water sports. Golf attractions range in price from $3.00 for nine putting holes to $4.00 for traditional miniature golf. Water sports range in price from $8.00 for a half hour of kayaking to $35.00 for a half hour on a wave runner. For information on golf attractions, call (919) 261–4900. For information on water sports, call (919) 441–4400.

Diamond Shoals Family Fun Park, also located on Highway 158 in Kill Devil Hills, was developed through innovative natural grass putting courses. Now the park has grown to include boats, water slides, a batting stadium, and a kiddie pool. You can also grab a snack at Flipper's Snack Bar. The batting stadium and golf courses are open from spring through fall. Water attractions are open mid-May through Labor Day. Prices range from $5.00 for miniature golf to $10.00 per day for the water slides. Call (919) 480–3553 for more information.

COROLLA

It's a little out of the way, but a drive up Highway 12 to this northernmost point on the North Carolina coast may prove very relaxing. The Corolla area is one of the narrowest points on the barrier islands. Bordered on the west by Currituck Sound and the Atlantic Ocean on the east, sand frequently blows onto the highway from the dunes that line it here and at other narrow points on the island. Highway 12 ends at the **Currituck Beach Lighthouse,** a red brick tower built in 1875. It is open for climbing for a $3.00 per person admission fee, which is used to help complete its renovation. It's open from Easter through Thanksgiving, from 10:00 A.M. to 6:00 P.M. daily.

CRESWELL

Now that we've explored the length of the Outer Banks, let's head back inland. Highway 64 is the quickest and easiest route out of the centrally located Manteo area. About 60 miles west of Manteo you come to **Pettigrew State Park** on Phelps Lake. The park includes 17,000 acres and plenty of room for camping, hiking, and fishing or picnicking on your way off the coast. You will want to see **Somerset Place State Historic Site** while you are at the park. Somerset is a fourteen-room manor built in the 1830s for Josiah Collins III from Somerset, England. The rice plantation and Greek Revival mansion became a popular gathering place for the upper class of the times and serve as an example of the South's slave-supported economy. Somerset, which houses an extensive collection of slave records, is the site of a homecoming for descendants of slaves and slaveholders. In recent years, a number of Indian artifacts have been pulled from the lake. Two dugout canoes, possibly 4,000 years old, are on display year-round, but more of the artifacts and history are presented during **Indian Heritage Week,** held at Pettigrew the third week in September. During the week schoolchildren from the area are presented with the history of the Algonquin Indians, who were wiped out by European-imported disease; the public is welcome on the weekend. During Indian Heritage Week you'll be able to view artifacts as well as get a chance to see how the Algonquin made many of the tools, pottery, and jewelry. Admission to the park is free, and it is open during daylight hours. For more information, call (919) 797–4475.

WILLIAMSTON

Staying on Highway 64 brings you west to this agriculturally based town that offers lessons in history and nature. There's plenty for sporting enthusiasts, who come here for the Roanoke River, but the town is also the home of **Morningstar Nature Refuge.** The naturalist-in-residence offers guided tours by appointment only, daily, throughout the year, or you can look around by yourself. Admission is free. Call (919) 792–7788 to learn more.

In 1995 the North Carolina Department of Agriculture broke ground on the **Eastern North Carolina Agricultural Center,** a multimillion-dollar equestrian center with a covered arena, outdoor rings, a cross-country course, and boarding facilities. The state operates the center in conjunction with the Martin Community College Equine Technology Program and plans special events throughout the year. For more information call the college at (919) 792–1521.

HAMILTON

To reach Hamilton, veer north from Williamston on State Highway 125. Most people who come here come to visit **Fort Branch,** an earthen Civil War fort, located on State Road 1416. On display are eight of the fort's original twelve cannons, which Confederate soldiers pushed into the Roanoke River after General Lee surrendered at Appomattox in 1865. The **Fort Branch Civil War Re-enactment** is held the first weekend in

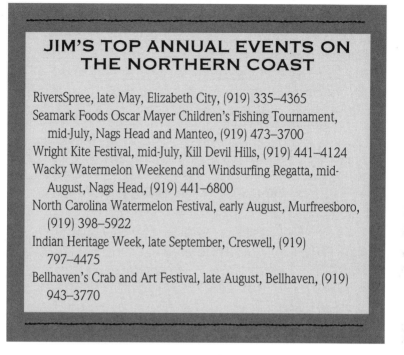

JIM'S TOP ANNUAL EVENTS ON THE NORTHERN COAST

RiversSpree, late May, Elizabeth City, (919) 335–4365

Seamark Foods Oscar Mayer Children's Fishing Tournament, mid-July, Nags Head and Manteo, (919) 473–3700

Wright Kite Festival, mid-July, Kill Devil Hills, (919) 441–4124

Wacky Watermelon Weekend and Windsurfing Regatta, mid-August, Nags Head, (919) 441–6800

North Carolina Watermelon Festival, early August, Murfreesboro, (919) 398–5922

Indian Heritage Week, late September, Creswell, (919) 797–4475

Bellhaven's Crab and Art Festival, late August, Bellhaven, (919) 943–3770

November, and the **Fort Branch Spring Living History Program** is another intriguing event this site offers. The fort is open from 1:30 to 5:30 P.M. Saturday and Sunday. Call (800) 776–8566 for more information.

ROBERSONVILLE

Back on Highway 64 heading west from Williamston, you can really pick up the pace if stock car racing is your thing. Races are held at the **East Carolina Motor Speedway,** a mile west of Robersonville on Highway 64, each Saturday night from April through November. Call (919) 795–4250 for more information.

TARBORO

Tarboro, west from Robersonville on Highway 64 at the juncture with Highway 258, is another town with its roots grounded deeply in the history of the eighteenth century. It's a prime location to study the architecture of the period, both in the charming downtown area and on the historic walking tour. The sixteen-acre Town Commons includes an 1860 cotton press and the **Blount-Bridgers House.** The house features the work of artist Hobson Pittman (1899–1972), whose works have been in collections at the Metropolitan Museum of Art in New York as well as the Corcoran Gallery in Washington, D.C. The house is open from April through November from 10:00 A.M. to 4:00 P.M. Monday through Friday and 2:00 to 4:00 P.M. Saturday and Sunday. Admission is $2.00 for adults and free for children through age eleven. For more information call (919) 823–4159.

ROCKY MOUNT

The city of Rocky Mount is a great stopping point on the way to or from the beach. You can get here from Tarsboro via Highway 64, heading west. From the north or south, Interstate 95 crosses the city's western edge. Numerous other roads also converge here. Stop at **Sunset Park** on River Drive, where you can take a break from the driving and have a picnic. You'll also find a miniature train here as well as a merry-go-round. Also on the park grounds is the **Rocky Mount Children's Museum,** which presents science demonstrations and planetarium shows. Live animals, including alligators, turtles, snakes, and ferrets, are also on display. Admission is free. The museum is open from 10:00 A.M. to 5:00 P.M. Monday through Friday, noon to 5:00 P.M. Saturday, and 2:00 to 5:00 P.M. Sunday. Call (919) 972–1167 for more information.

WILSON

Head south on Highway 301 to the town of Wilson, not only one of the state's premier barbecue locales, but also the home of **Imagination Station,** at 224 East Nash Street. After grabbing a bite at one of the several restaurants recognized by *Southern Living* for their quality barbecue beef, pork, and chicken, head to this unusual science center with exhibits that will make your hair stand on end. Included are daily science demonstrations on everything from chemistry to electricity, a state of the art computer lab, and dozens of hands-on exhibits. Admission is $3.50 for adults, $3.00 for people ages four through seventeen, and free for children under four. The museum is open from 10:00 A.M. to 6:00 P.M. Monday through Saturday and from 1:00 to 5:00 P.M. Sunday. Call (919) 291–5113 for more information.

WINDSOR

If you choose to head north instead of west from Williamston, you can take Highway 17 to reach Windsor. **Livermon Recreational Park and Mini-Zoo** at Granville and York streets is a great place to stop if you're on the road. Take along the makings for a picnic (grills are available if you want to cook hot dogs or hamburgers) and let the kids run off some steam on the playground equipment. They can also tour the little zoo and see the thirty different varieties of animals, including birds, goats, and a llama. The zoo offers a rare opportunity to see the animals up close and even pet some of them. The park is open from 8:00 A.M. to 8:00 P.M. Monday through Friday, 9:00 A.M. to 8:00 P.M. Saturday and Sunday during the summer and from 8:00 A.M. to 5:00 P.M. daily during the winter. Admission is free. Call (919) 794–5553 for more information.

If you've taken a ferry on your trip to the Outer Banks or you're getting ready to, drop by and see the **Sans Soucie Ferry** on the Cashie River. The ferry isn't marked on state maps, but you can find it by taking State Highway 308 East. Go about 10 miles and take a right on State Road 1500. The ferry is one of three surviving two-car inland river ferries in North Carolina. It's open daily, and crossing is free.

Go west on Highway 308 about 4 miles and you'll find the **Historic Hope Plantation.** This home of David Stone, one of North Carolina's governors, features an extensive library and a fabulous collection of eighteenth- and nineteenth-century furniture. The complex is open March 1 through December 23 from 10:00 A.M. to 4:00 P.M. Monday through Saturday and 2:00 to 5:00 P.M. Sunday. Admission costs $5.00 for adults and $1.75 for children ages five through eighteen. Call (919) 794–3140 for more information.

MURFREESBORO

Historic Murfreesboro, located farther north at the intersection of Highways 258 and 158, has been painstakingly restored to its eighteenth- and nineteenth-century condition. "Renaissance in North Carolina" is one of the country's most ambitious renovation projects. More than twenty buildings have been restored in this river port town, and five (at press time) are open to the public. Tours of the district are available starting at 116 East Main Street from 8:30 A.M. to noon and 1:00 to 5:00 P.M. Monday, Tuesday, Thursday, and Friday. For more information, call (919) 398–5922. Ask about the annual **Watermelon Festival** held in the summer and about **Colonial Christmas.**

GATESVILLE

If you and your family love nature, you'll want to stop at the **Merchant Millpond State Park** near Gatesville. The park is accessible via Highways 158, 32, and 37, but you rarely find big crowds here. With more than 2,900 acres, there is more than enough elbow room. The main feature is a millpond created when the gristmill and dam were constructed in 1811. You'll love canoeing through some of North Carolina's oldest Cyprus trees, some that may be well over 1,000 years old. Canoes are available by the hour, day, or overnight—if you are ready to rough it in the park's canoe-in campground. You can also fish and hike, or you can enjoy one of the interpretive nature programs offered by the park. The park is open during daylight hours. Call (919) 357–1191 for more information.

EDENTON

To continue your trip, take Highway 37 to Highway 32 south to Edenton. Located at the head of Albemarle Sound, this place has been called one of the prettiest towns in the South, and as soon as you drive in, you'll see why. History abounds here, as it does in many of the coastal communities. Today, Edenton is largely a retirement community, and many of the inns won't accommodate younger children. The scenery and history, however, make it worth the stop. Two-hour guided tours of **Historic Edenton** are offered daily, beginning at the visitor center at 108 North Broad Street. On the tour you will see the 1782 home of Penelope Barker, who organized the Edenton Tea Party in which fifty-one local women showed their support for banning consumption of British Tea. It was considered one of the first occasions when women took part in a political act. In addition, the tour will show you the **Chowan County Courthouse** (circa 1767), a very distinguished building from the time; the **James Iredell House** (circa 1773), the residence of one member of the first U.S. Supreme Court; and the **Cupola House,** (circa 1758), the state's oldest remaining wooden structure. The tours cost $12 per family. Call (919) 482–2637 for more information.

HERTFORD

Staying on Highway 17 takes you to State Road 1336 and to the **Newbold-White House.** The oldest brick house in North Carolina, it was built in 1685. The home has been restored to mint condition and is decorated with seventeenth-century furnishings. A small admission fee is charged for guided tours of the house, which is open from March 1 to Thanksgiving, from 10:00 A.M. to 4:30 P.M. Monday through Saturday. Call (919) 426–7567 for more information.

As you travel farther east on Highway 17, you come to a rather obscure attraction. The **S-shaped Bridge** is the only bridge of its kind in the country. Built in 1929, it was constructed to replace a floating bridge that historians have dated to 1798.

ELIZABETH CITY

On Highway 17 you can head east to Elizabeth City. The chamber of commerce (919–335–4365) can provide you with a map for a historical walking tour as well as information on the Albemarle Sound area. But if you do nothing else here, see the **Museum of the Albemarle,** 1116 Highway 17 South. This branch of the North Carolina Museum of History provides a fine overview, from prehistoric times to the present, of the all-important waterway and the ten counties that surround it. Here you will see Indian relics and other artifacts from the region. Admission is free. The museum is open from 9:00 A.M. to 5:00 P.M. Tuesday through Saturday and 2:00 to 5:00 P.M. Sunday.

General Index

ACTIVITIES INDEXES

MUSEUMS

SPORTS/PARKS/OUTDOOR RECREACTION

FESTIVALS AND CELEBRATIONS